WINNING PR IN THE WIRED WORLD

WINNING PR IN THE WIRED WORLD

POWERFUL COMMUNICATIONS STRATEGIES FOR THE NOISY DIGITAL SPACE

Don Middleberg

McGraw-Hill

New York   San Francisco   Washington, D.C.   Auckland   Bogotá
Caracas   Lisbon   London   Madrid   Mexico City   Milan
Montreal   New Delhi   San Juan   Singapore
Sydney   Tokyo   Toronto

Library of Congress Cataloging-in-Publication Data

Middleberg, Don.
    Winning PR in the wired world / Don Middleberg.
       p.   cm.
    ISBN 0-07-136342-4 (acid-free paper)
    1. Public relations.   2. Internet in public relations.   I. Title.

    HM1221.M53   2001
    659.2—ds21   00-045080

McGraw-Hill

A Division of The **McGraw·Hill** Companies

1 2 3 4 5 6 7 8 9 0 DOC/DOC 0 9 8 7 6 5 4 3 2 1 0

ISBN 0-07-136342-4

Printed and bound by R. R. Donnelley & Sons Company.

McGraw-Hill books are available at special quantity discounts to use as premiums and sales promotions, or for use in corporate training programs. For more information, please write to the Director of Special Sales, Professional Publishing, McGraw-Hill, Two Penn Plaza, New York, NY 10121-2298. Or contact your local bookstore.

This book is printed on recycled, acid-free paper containing a minimum of 50% recycled, de-inked fiber.

To my wife Sande, who was there for me when I most needed her love, faith, support, and especially her great sense of humor. And to the two shining lights of my life, my daughters Melissa and Stephanie.

CONTENTS

PREFACE

The Internet is the most powerful, most global, and most revolutionary communications medium in the history of the world. Its impact changes everything, including public relations, forever and for the better. It forces massive rethinking of all that we do. In short, the Internet changes the very nature of business.

Not long ago, Smith Corona, the venerable old typewriter company, was delisted from the National Association of Securities Dealers Quotations (NASDAQ) exchange after its market capitalization dived below $5 million. A really tragic ending to a once great company; one that looked like it was on the cutting edge, ready to take over the world. Smith Corona dominated the office machines market for years. Its typewriters helped many students get through college. Now, $25 on eBay gets you a museum piece. The moral of the story is that no business can live on past laurels. Was there a more aptly named book than Andy Grove's *Only the Paranoid Survive?*

Without question, many of today's Internet companies will meet the same fate as Smith Corona. In fact, less than half of the *Fortune 500* companies in the last century are still part of it today, and many are no longer in business. These are companies that failed to keep up with change.

For public relations professionals, the message is simple: don't change, and you will face the consequences. Embrace the new digital world and you will thrive along with it.

Back in the early 1990s, I talked myself blue in the face, trying to get public relations professionals to understand the coming significance of the Internet. I would threaten, cajole, scream, do just about anything in my talks before the Public Relations Society of America (PRSA). I would start my discussions by asking two questions: Who among you thinks the Internet is the most overhyped, overused, most abused medium you have ever heard of? And who among you thinks the Internet is the most underhyped, underused, most misunderstood medium you have overused? Well, you could virtually plot the responses on a time line. In the early to mid-1990s virtually everyone in the room shot their hands to the sky, all knowing the Internet would be a flash in the pan, an annoyance to put up with until things returned to normal. To my second question, a few intrepid souls meekly put their hands up, embarrassed to even think that way. Thankfully, there were always two or three (out of a hundred or so) who would get it. Their hands would go up with a knowing smile. My response to these groups has always been the same: "I'm with the second group. And for those of you in the first group who continue to feel that way—over the next few years, you will be guilty of public relations incompetence." Suddenly, I got their attention. By the end of the presentation, the line of people waiting to speak to me would often stretch 20 people deep.

Nothing has so radically and fundamentally changed the way public relations professionals approach their tasks as has the Internet. In the 1980s, the fax machine was the technology breakthrough that allowed public relations professionals to get their messages out immediately. Press releases and media advisories could be sent to top media contacts for timely follow-up, while a standard press release mailing through the U.S. Postal Service reached the masses. The fax was, and remains, a simple medium that helped public relations professionals garner quick results. But the Internet is an entirely different animal.

At both the corporate and government levels, the democratization of technology, finance, and information started to converge in the late 1980s and created amazing new efficiencies and economies of scale, a whole new place to do business really, and it was called *cyberspace*. This transformation became known as the Information Revolution, and it will be seen in time as one of those great leaps forward in technology that occur every hundred years, like electricity. What resulted was a lowering of the barriers to enter a marketplace to virtually zero and radically increased competition, as did the speed by which a product was moved from being an innovation to a commodity.

Edward Yardeni, chief economist for Deutsche Bank, has pointed out that the Internet is the closest thing in the world today to the model of perfect competition. In the model of perfect competition, he notes, "there are no barriers to entry, no protection from failure for unprofitable firms, and everyone (consumers and producers) has easy and free access to all information. These just happen to be the three main characteristics of Internet commerce. . . . The Internet lowers the cost of comparison shopping to zero. Increasingly, the consumer can easily and quickly find the lowest price for any good or service. In the cyber-economy, the low-cost producer will offer the lowest price and provide this information at no cost to any and all potential customers anywhere on the planet." In the low-tech economy, notes Yardeni, the cost of searching for the lowest price was relatively high. You had to climb over all sorts of walls and travel all sorts of distances to get the best deal, and this gave a built-in advantage to local or well-established companies and stores. Now, manufacturers, service providers, or retailers anywhere in the world can bid for business anywhere in the world. That's why it's going to be wonderful to be a consumer in the age of the Internet, and it's going to be hell on wheels to be a producer.

In the last several years, the Internet has evolved more rapidly as a communications medium than anything that has gone before it. And with more and more consumers and businesses going online, there's no ignoring it. This unprecedented medium is bringing public relations professionals together with the media, customers, employees, and investors online, 24 hours a day, 7 days a week. But because of its evolving nature and the sheer possibilities of using it as a public relations tool, the Internet has been a difficult medium for public relations professionals to wrap their arms around.

Public relations is no longer just about "ink." It's about a brilliant idea, creatively communicated by traditional and new media, in entirely new ways.

We are inspired to change the very core of what we do. Inspired to think differently. Inspired to change the fundamental nature of our business.

We are living in the greatest time in our history. It is truly the Golden Age of public relations. All we have to do is act. But you better move fast because another 50,000 folks are on the Internet since you started reading this book.

Those in my firm will tell you that I quote from my grandmother a great deal. Lacking a formal education, she was easily the smartest person I ever met and the most courageous. Imagine being 14 in the early 1900s, being put on a boat to a foreign country, and merely given the equivalent of $5 and the address of an uncle living on the lower East Side of New York City. My grandmother knew more about communications than anyone I have ever met. I even think Marshall McLuhan's famous phrase, "the medium is the message," was plagiarized from my grandmother. She gave me a message I'd like to share with you. At least 100 times, she said, "Donald (she was the only person who ever called me Donald), it's not just what you say, it is how you say it." Amen, Grandma.

This book will provide you with real strategies and techniques used by top public relations professionals working in the digital world. We will get into the significant, albeit limited, research done to date. We will look at the successes and abysmal failures. You will read how cutting-edge companies are making their mark in the online and offline worlds. What you do with this information is entirely up to you. But for Pete's sake, do something. Apart from face-to-face interaction, no communications technique has ever allowed people to say things more creatively, expressively, precisely, and powerfully than the Internet. It's changed the world of communications. Now let's see how we can capture its secrets to make it work for you.

ACKNOWLEDGMENTS

My sincerest thanks to agency principal and temporary book project manager Amy Jackson for her invaluable work on this project. How she put up with me during the book development period I still don't know. A special thanks to Hope Galvin, an extraordinarily "street smart" lady who has stood by me for 20 years. To Bethany Sherman, Curtis Hougland, Neil Vineberg, and Chris Hayes for serving as my agency partners with patience, grace, smarts, and unbridled enthusiasm. To my new partner, Bob Schmetterer, CEO of Euro RSCG, it's going to be a great adventure for the both of us. To associate professor Steve Ross for our wonderful 6-year partnership, resulting in the "Middleberg/Ross Media in Cyberspace" research studies. I would also like to recognize friends and associates whom I have been fortunate enough to work with over the years. People like Ray Gaulke, COO of the Public Relations Society of America, Jack Bergen, president of The Council of Public Relations Firms, and Paul Holmes, publisher of *Inside PR*, a man who has been totally supportive of the public relations industry. And to my agency friends like Margie Booth, Steve Cody, Connie Conners, David Drobis, Cathy Lugbauer, Ken Makovsky, David Paine, and Gerry Schwartz, among others. I know how hard you work, how professionally you serve your clients, and how caring you are to your people. A special thank you to my editor Michelle Reed, and my agents at Kim Witherspoon Associates, Kim Witherspoon and David Forrer.

And to all the "Middlebergers" through the years whose hard work, creativity, and passion for this business remain a daily inspiration and whose personalities and humor add joy to everything we do together.

INTRODUCTION

Today's world of digital public relations has happened quickly, but not overnight. At times, public relations has lagged behind the rapid transformations of both entrepreneurs and *Fortune 500* companies. And at other times, public relations has lead the charge. Clearly, there have been individuals, specific companies, and agencies that have helped to carve the path that others have followed. But there still is the opportunity to forge a new direction, one that leads to results never before imagined. Many of those early trailblazers who cleared new paths with hard work and risk have realized the bottom-line results: higher stock values, enhanced employee and customer loyalty, and professional and personal growth. But it was not accomplished without some growing pains.

The evolution of digital public relations can really be dated to the 1970s, when the use of electronic bulletin boards and news distribution first took hold. At that point, non-governmental organizations first began using services such as PeaceNet to receive and repackage news electronically via feeds, and a small but loyal bulletin board audience began growing, using the computer to reach out to fellow Bulletin Board Service (BBS) users. Journalists and tech users alike logged on with phone modems to connect with others via Usenet and local BBS boards, often with the favorite machine of that moment, the Radio Shack TRS 80, an early personal computer whose ease of use and features were remarkably advanced for the time period.

The digital communications era that most closely resembles the world we know today began in the early 1990s, spawning the practice of digital public relations shortly thereafter. The evolution of that particular niche among the public relations community can be viewed in five stages:

1. *Not with my journalists*: Very few communication professionals could have anticipated how the Internet would revolutionize public relations in the early 1990s. Many met this new medium with suspicion, claiming that journalists would never adapt to this type of communication, and therefore dismissed it as an integral tool for their own profession. In a way, they were right. Public relations as we knew it to be at that point was already dead.

2. *Watch out, the Internet is out to get us*: Around 1995, when more and more communications professionals were beginning to recognize the potential power of the Internet, the pervasive tone became fear. Online publications were sprouting in the mainstream, most significantly with the three S's—Suck, Slate, and Salon—each with the power to instantly reach a whole new global audience. At that moment, Intel had just battled a costly public relations crisis with its Pentium chip, a crisis largely spawned by its own inattention to a complaint about a manufacturing error posted by a college professor in a Usenet newsgroup. The post became broadcast news in a matter of days, forcing Intel to recall the product and reconcile a three-point drop in its stock price on a single day. Andy Grove said that mistake cost Intel $500 million! Soon, other companies, such as Ford, Shell, and Cigna, began to field inquiries from reporters about online rumors. Many communications professionals and CEOs developed a fear that the Internet had become the most dangerous foe to corporate reputations since Ralph Nader. Most feared the dissemination of corporate secrets and skeletons, activist postings and campaigns, and remained blind to the potential opportunity to reach out to new audiences and develop more powerful relationships with current audiences.

3. *Look how cool we are*: Communicators soon recognized that journalists were indeed rapidly turning to the Internet. They also saw that other important business audiences, i.e., analysts, employees, customers, partners, and regulators, were getting

online. So professionals began to ask, "How do I bring my public relations program online?" Some began dabbling in web site development, and battled with their tech departments about ownership and control. Others sought to add e-mail, online press release distribution, and web sites to their current public relations processes and campaigns. But several *Fortune 500* companies were hesitant to move, paralyzed by issues of who owns the web site and what the web site was supposed to do for the company. The transformative power of the Internet on every fiber of business practice had yet to be recognized. It was a time when lots of communicators patted themselves on the back for merely knowing what a listserv was. Cutting edge was defined as the ability to put press releases on a web site and including online publications in media lists.

For many, the medium became the message. Hosting a Webcast held cachet. Communicators reported that their company images were changing in the eyes of the media because they had begun investing in technology to help reach out to these audiences, sometimes without any truly new business initiatives to support these new "savvy" reputations. Public relations agencies began using e-mail to blast news to reporters and mass audiences, and the word *SPAM* entered the vocabulary. Journalists who had just started to embrace e-mail now were reluctant to log on to download hundreds of mass e-mails that had little use beyond cluttering the in box. Coupled with the slow connectivity through sources like AOL and Compuserv, these circumstances bred a journalist backlash and short-lived slowdown in digital public relations.

4. *Rethinking the public relations organization*: By 1996, smart, innovative communicators looked at this backlash and began to rethink what "digital public relations" really meant. The Internet wasn't just a tool—the Internet could completely transform entire communications processes, changing the dynamics internally between the company and its current audience and even between businesses. Large companies, from financial behemoths to entertainment moguls, began to invest in training. They hired outside help to infuse Internet knowledge into their communications teams and educate management as to how

these investments could help keep organizations competitive. Companies such as Duke Energy and Bell Atlantic adopted Internet steering committees. There, communications professionals met regularly with leaders from technology, marketing, customer relations, business units, and global divisions, ensuring that they were truly diffusing Internet culture and communications throughout the organization. At the same time, new brands were emerging on the market, including CDNow and TheStreet.com. These new, successful brands helped keep the larger organizations on their toes for new ways to compete.

5. *Full communications transformation*: Today, digital communications is the grease that keeps a fully networked, rapidly changing organization moving quickly, strategically, and intelligently. Large-scale public relations departments have reinvented themselves to truly meld wireless and wired communications into the way they do business. Responsiveness and innovation are king—change is the only true constant. No longer do public relations organizations designate certain employees as "the Internet folks." Now, all levels of employees understand and execute strategies based in the wired world. Smaller organizations have created a utopia where marketing, advertising, and public relations are truly integrated—an opportunity the Internet birthed.

CEOs, CFOs, and CIOs are investing in public relations like never before. Those organizations that have reallocated budgets and resources to harness the power of digital public relations have seen improved speed to market, enhanced awareness among key communities, and better results on the bottom line. Countless public relations executives have slashed costs by fully transforming their communications processes and relying on digital production and transfer of communications materials. These new communications organizations are able to move at remarkable speed, redefining corporate doctrine every 90 days and responding to change as necessary.

Of course, there are still holdouts, even in today's environment. Clinging to tradition, they insist on even more proof of the efficiency of the wired world. Those who have successfully completed the full-scale communications transformation have usually demonstrated several levels of understanding:

1. *Management that "gets it"*: No company has ever been successful in transforming its communications practices without the commitment of key management. A company like Intel has understood, especially since their 1994 Pentium chip scare, that a well-oiled, highly resourced public relations machine will allow them to move quickly in a fast-moving space.

2. *Internal leadership*: Every successful communications organization has leaders who have sought to rock the boat and diffuse new ideas throughout the organization. They have embraced internal and external resources, and are committed to deploying them in their organization.

3. *The ability to take risks*: No precedents have been set in the world of digital public relations without risk taking. Those who need to follow a manual have been left behind. Take About.com, which did a brilliant job of rebranding itself. Originally called "The Mining Company," it changed its name to better reflect who it was and what it did. To do so, it launched a well-known grassroots, online, and print campaign, titled "Is anybody out there?" The campaign was designed to promote use of real, live site guides, which helped rebrand the company. The rebranding eventually led to a relatively successful IPO. And About.com is consistently among the top 10 visited sites.

4. *The courage to constantly destroy and create*: Former Apple executive Guy Kawasaki said in his oft-referenced book, *Rules for Revolutionaries*, that organizations need to eat like a bird and poop like an elephant. Kawasaki meant that companies need to constantly pursue new ideas, identify those practices that are working well, and quickly discard those that are not efficient.

5. *An understanding that business is moving as fast as communications*: Some companies have been caught in the wheel of

rebranding without the business transformation to back it up. Entertainment organizations have been particularly prone to trouble, finding it hard to balance an image of cool, smart, and savvy with old-line policies toward image rights management and adoption of online entertainment opportunities.

Organizations that have developed and will continue to create the future of digital public relations are diverse and have contributed in different ways. Old companies transitioning to the digital world faced special challenges. They needed to redefine and reintroduce their brands, yet had to do so quickly because well-funded new brands were constantly entering the market. Some did it better than others. General Motors is enjoying a new renaissance despite entries from players like CarsDirect and AutoWeb.com. That's because a new focus by a few key leaders was able to pull the company out of the 1950s and into the twenty-first century. *Most recently, GM announced that it would establish a new site that would sell all cars, not just its own brands. The reason: get close to and, if possible, capture the young customer for life.* Other established companies took a different tack by creating new companies and spinning them off. Book giant Barnes and Noble opted to form new businesses, such as BarnesandNoble.com. This allowed them to leverage existing brand dominance coupled with new brand infusion, balancing old- and new-world qualities and practices. And brands such as Intel, Microsoft, and Cisco have managed to neatly face the special challenge of keeping cool, keeping hip, and keeping momentum over especially long periods of market dominance. In the future, more brands will exhibit this sort of communications maturity as they move from emerging to established player status.

In all cases, the established companies reacted appropriately to the changing market conditions. Their very survival depends on it. New companies, such as AppGenesys, Video ASP, VastVideo, and Voice ASP Intraco, have moved so quickly, developing new communication methods as part and parcel of discovering new ways of doing business in today's economy, that they pose an immediate challenge. Although most haven't been

around a long time, the speed of today's market brought them
to the point of taking on the establishment much faster than
they would have even 5 years ago.

Those who prefer to bury their proverbial heads in the sand
and wait until the "wave" passes risk not only their professional
careers, but also the health and opportunities for the brands
and businesses within their sphere. These dinosaurs have a lot
to lose. The credibility of an organization is often predicated on
its ability to adapt to changing times. Would you invest in a
brand that has no Internet strategy or one that is executing on
it with new hires, new initiatives, and new practices? Doubtful.
Playing catch-up is often more risky than being part of the first
wave. If you're a worker for one of these slow-moving corporations, you risk being seen as part of a group that simply doesn't
understand the business climate, an extremely bad mark on
someone's career.

The communicator inside you must ask: Who hasn't highlighted experiences within the digital economy on his or her
résumé? And who has seen Internet-savvy peers, competitors,
and colleagues get ahead? Who has been invited to meetings
and/or included in projects because of their experience on the
Internet? And it goes much deeper than that. Because of the
speedy changes in business, today's giant may be tomorrow's
memory. What has happened to the Toys 'R' Us market share?
And what about once dominant Xerox? Answer: it's being eaten
by smaller, more nimble competitors who got into the wired
world early and quickly learned its lessons.

The problems of being late to the game seem to snowball the
longer they are in place. Why does Scient receive so many
résumés? It's perceived as a forward-thinking company with a
future. Why does Andersen Consulting face a bleeding employee
force? Everyone wants to be a part of what they perceive as a
winning strategy. Finally, ask yourself: how many companies are
losing business customers to those who can help improve business efficiency? How can an organization compete when it can't
accelerate its own business processes, much less those of its customers? The answer is obvious. The Internet is here to stay. And

those that do not learn its lessons are in danger of being left on the dock.

Some books have attempted to address the needs of an audience interested in exploring the bold new frontier of the wired world with tactical "how-to" texts on Internet marketing and publicity. But most of those attempts have focused on adding Internet tactics to offline public relations programs. Thus, up-and-coming graduate and undergraduate students must rely on published research, articles, and web sites to get their grounding in the digital communications principles and concepts. Such tactics have mostly been akin to poking a stick into a dark room and learning through experience. And it hasn't been a pleasant experience for a lot of them.

This book is organized into chapters focusing on specific tactics and strategies for communicating in the digital economy. Chapter 1 should be used to orient oneself and to provide a background into the world of digital public relations, how we've gotten to where we are today, and why it is an important medium to explore. In Chapter 2, we look at the Four Fast Rules of Communicating in the Digital Age. These must-have rules are the guidelines for defining and exhibiting the best practices in e-communications. In Chapter 3, we look closely at how the roles of advertising and public relations have changed due to the exaggerated role public relations has been asked to play in building brands.

In Chapter 4, we look at how organizations have—and must—redefine themselves and practice "continuous rebranding" in order to stay competitive. Chapters 5, 6, and 7 focus on the new players that have redefined their roles in today's public relations. Media has changed not only how they work but also who they are and what they do. Therefore, the role of media relations has become both more important and has completely changed the routine of the public relations executive. Chapter 6 explores the new audiences that have increased in importance, including analysts, investors, and employees. The chapter explores not only why they are important but also what they demand of the new e-communicator. Chapter 7 identifies a new business player, the celebrity CEO, and identifies the new challenges for the public relations professional trying to build that cachet.

Chapters 8, 9, 10, and 11 introduce the new challenges the Internet has brought to companies to stay competitive: online image managemen, crisis communications, viral communications online, and intelligence gathering. Professionals need to master these three areas in order to bring their public relations programs up to speed.

Chapter 12 outlines the ways these new rules of communication can be measured and demonstrated through a close look at one of the most successful Internet launches in history, Britannica.com. The author concludes with some of his own projections for trends we will see emerge in public relations as the next few years unfold.

Together, these chapters will provide an overview of where public relations professionals have been and where they're heading: directly to a world of ubiquitous communications, where the ability to react to constant change is the only method that will ensure an individual's and a corporation's long-term survival.

PUBLIC RELATIONS: YOU'VE COME A LONG WAY, BABY

There was once a public relations executive who was running a very small, 10-person public relations firm that had maybe a half-dozen clients.

He was trying to figure out how in the world he could compete against the public relations giants of the world, the Burson Marstellers and the Hill & Knowltons. They were killing him every time he went out for a pitch.

This executive was not landing the accounts because his staff wasn't as good as the staffs at the giants or because his ideas for campaigns weren't innovative and cost-effective.

They were beating him because many CEOs didn't want to take any risks. Many potential clients said to him, "I'm not taking any chances. I'm hiring the biggest firm. I don't care what they cost."

That wasn't necessarily the best decision. But, admittedly, there was less risk in deciding bigger was better.

So this same executive was sitting around his office one day in 1993 when he received a call from J. P. Donlon, who was in charge of *Chief Executive* magazine. Donlon asked to have a manuscript that the executive was writing for a client sent over. But instead of sending it over on paper, Donlon asked that the executive put it on a disk.

At the time, the executive had one 286-megahertz computer in his office. So he put his 5¼-inch floppy disk in the drive, copied the story onto the disk, and delivered the floppy by messenger to Donlon, who was, by now, thinking he was the coolest editor in the country.

Shortly after that, the executive received a phone call from another fellow named Andy Glueck, who was a senior editor of *Worth* magazine. Glueck was calling to cancel a luncheon to be held that day. He was going to come into New York City from Long Island, but told the executive that he was no longer coming into Manhattan.

The guy with the 10-person agency asked, facetiously, "You mean, ever?"

Glueck came right back at him. "Right. I am never coming into Manhattan again. I am going to do all my interviews over the phone or online. Then I'm typing my stories online and sending them in online." It seems *Worth* magazine had wired his house for him.

It was at that point that the lightbulb went off and the public relations executive realized that something significant was happening. He realized that if he came to understand how journalists were now using the Internet as a way to do their jobs, and could develop new ways to reach these journalists, he might have a way to finally compete against the Burson Marstellers of the world.

So right then and there that executive—yours truly—decided to plunge headlong into the wired world, becoming one of the first agencies to embrace the digital space.

It worked.

Diving into the world of the Internet's convergence with established media wasn't easy. For one, there was no real roadmap at that time on how the changing climate was affecting the public relations business.

So one of the initial ways my public relations agency and some other public relations specialists began to take the first baby steps toward adapting to journalists like Donlon and Glueck was to ask whether they were reflecting a trend.

My own experiences with a handful of media in the early 1990s indicated that the ways of researching and writing a story, as well as publishing the results, were starting to change.

Sure, it was interesting that a handful of young, savvy technology journalists in New York were using "the information superhighway." But what was going on in the rest of the country?

Unfortunately, there was no body of research that looked at these developing practices on a national scale. Even at the renowned Columbia University Graduate School of Journalism, no formal studies had been conducted in the area of online journalism.

In fact, in 1994, only one Columbia professor thought this was an area even worth looking into.

His name was Steven Sanders Ross.

Ross was a long-time technology addict, electronic bulletin board user, and proponent of introducing his students to the newest trends in computer-assisted reporting. When he was contacted for research on the developing world of online journalism, he admitted that little existed. But he quickly agreed to move forward on conducting the first formal investigation.

Thus, the Middleberg/Ross Media in Cyberspace Study was founded in 1994 not only to educate my own 10-person firm but also to begin educating the public relations industry as to how savvy professionals could do their jobs more effectively by incorporating the Internet into everything they did.

The first results were released in the spring of that year at a Public Relations Society of America (PRSA) conference, and became an instant sensation.

Remember, at that time, the commercial Internet barely existed, and was still largely regarded as the province of scientists, the military, and hobbyists.

So the PRSA audience at that 1994 conference was shocked to discover that as many as 17 percent of journalists at that moment admitted to using the Internet as a research tool.

For the first time, there was information available that showed public relations professionals and the companies they represented how critical the Internet was becoming for the way they did business. The Internet was not only for academics and geeks. It was rapidly transforming into an essential business tool.

From that moment forward, there was a greater understanding among public relations firms and others of the challenges and opportunities facing the emerging community of online entrepreneurs.

Such understanding was greatly needed. Many of the early Internet pioneers—particularly people such as Andy Klein of Wit Capital, SonicNet founder Tim Nye, and AdOne founder Steve Brotman—felt that many public relations agencies of that time period did not understand the urgency of the Internet as well as they did.

With organizations beginning to spring up, such as the World Wide Web Artists' Consortium (WWWAC) and Aliza Sherman's Webgrrls, and journalists beginning to emerge, such as Lisa Napoli at Cybertimes and Mo Krochmal at TechWeb, an energy bigger than anyone imagined was being created—a force, a driving focus, that was going to change public relations forever. Some agency veterans will tell you they were asleep at the wheel during the Internet revolution. While these individuals continued to conduct business as usual, they let a whole new generation of public relations practitioners emerge as the true powers of the profession. Times changed fast, too fast for many senior executives who were used to conducting business as usual. After all, until the Internet came into being, public relations was arguably a pretty sleepy business.

In the old days, public relations was consigned to a list of priorities that ranked somewhere around having the executive washroom fully stocked with paper and making sure "the boys" had a fully stocked bar at night. That's particularly hard to believe for many young public relations executives, many of whom have never lived through a recession. But public relations can partly blame itself for such perceptions.

It is easy to see why it was not highly regarded when its early practices are examined. The profession previously relied a great deal on the type of bombast that appeals to a less-than-highbrow audience.

Public relations, as an industry, started in entertainment, in movies, and on Broadway. Theater producers would put a bikini-clad model in a leopard-skin Cadillac and have her go down Broadway and give out theater tickets. And, oh yes, call the papers and get a photo-op. It was hucksterism, trying to get people to stick their nose into the circus tent to take a look. It was a hard hustle, done by men who sat elbow to elbow in the saloons with the writers. That's why many of them were referred to as *press agents*, because that's literally what they did, selling items to columnists.

Of course, that led to a definite lack of respect and certainly very low fees. Professionalism was something the other guy did.

The notion that public relations was more than flackery began to change as the rise of the multinational corporation made it part of the business world. That was the era of excruciatingly slow communications.

A client would call and say, "I'd like to go over this press release now."

The public relations executive, again yours truly, would reply, "I'm sorry. It didn't come in today's mail. I'm sure it will come tomorrow."

And then he and his buddies at the agency would hang up and go back to playing darts. Today's young professionals can't even imagine a world so slow paced and leisurely. Before the Internet, there was also a certain mentality that existed that insisted it was okay to do anything to get a story. That's not to say everyone in public relations didn't have ethics. But the mentality was different because the world of the saloon-bred press agent allowed them to play around with their events. There was more scheming and plotting. Yes, it was fun. But it certainly wasn't much of a profession.

Today, the marketplace depends upon credibility. You have to be truthful, or you get flamed out of business.

Even as it gradually moved from hucksterism and press stunts, public relations still wasn't attuned to anything close to the world of today.

When agencies used to get involved with strategic research in the 1980s and early 1990s, the approach was different. We'd sit around a room and say, "Here is the problem. What do we do about it?"

Everyone, inevitably, would say, "Let's do a study."

The Japanese were notoriously successful at this. They'd go out and conduct research and they would study a problem for several months at a clip, covering every little nuance. They would then come back with a document 4 inches thick, get the group together again, analyze it, and put together a public relations plan, also 4 inches thick, covering every conceivable event and action to take place over the next 3 years.

No one does strategic planning that way anymore, if they do it at all. Now it's all about speed. You don't have to be first to market, but if you do it better than your competitors and get their first, that's what it takes to win.

So the very nature of business has fundamentally changed because of the Internet, including public relations. Those firms and companies that understand are the winners. Technology makes forecasting impossible. Technology has changed public relations forever and for the better.

The early pioneers of the Internet grasped that. For those early companies, the Internet wasn't just another way to communicate—it was their mantra, their reason for being. And they needed public relations people who could adjust strategies on the fly, adopt new methodologies into their core business practices, and understand the language of technology.

A new medium that would become a part of the mainstream faster than any one that had come before was being created. There was no holding it back, and the public relations companies who realized that would quickly become the leaders of this emerging business.

This is truly the golden age of public relations, particularly for public relations practitioners who understand that, in the digital world that has emerged in the last 5 years, there has never been more opportunity. But great opportunity never comes without great risk.

To be successful using the Internet, it's important to know what the Internet is about and what it takes. It's more than just a lot of promises and a lot of hype. This is an expensive ballgame. It requires great management in addition to a solid business plan. And because it is so expensive, now is when people are at the greatest risk of losing it all if they make the wrong moves.

Essentially, public relations has been impacted by five important business communications trends catalyzed by the growth of the Internet: speed, access, new rules of interaction, brand redefinition, and business partners as currency. Public relations ability to respond instantly to these trends has embedded its status as business-critical—essential to companies that move quickly and need to maximize the impact of their cash outlays.

Let's examine each of those factors in public relations driving role in Internet business building. While they are distinct categories of measure, they combine to form an overall picture of today's Internet economy.

SPEED AND AGILITY

We live in an age where change comes at the click of a mouse, and requires companies to often react within hours to challenges that arise, both in the real world and from the sometimes anonymous world of the Internet. That's where public relations has a distinct advantage. It can react instantly, shifting to accommodate any schedule or news cycle. For public relations executives, the luxury of sitting back and planning a response over time is no longer possible. In fact, every minute that goes by can often make a problem worse or an opportunity disappear. Slow response practices can even allow false rumors and inaccuracies in stories to gain momentum, growing like kudzu and building upon bad or false information, to the point where a company is faced with answering questions about perceptions and bad information, in the process losing its focus and being perceived as evasive. Any response that isn't immediate and focused gives opponents—real and imagined—an advantage that can damage a company's image. We now live in a global information age, with Internet news outlets, worldwide broadcasting, and instant analysis. If something happens on a Saturday night at 10 p.m. pacific time, an eastern time zone company has to respond as rapidly and effectively as if the incident had happened on a Tuesday afternoon. That's almost unthinkable from what the situation would have been like even 5 years ago.

Strategic planning is dead. Now, this is an uncomfortable notion for the old guard. Many veteran business leaders were used to a much different process. The methodology they use is from a kinder, gentler age, one where contemplation and thoughtful reflection were the hallmarks of good business practice. If businesses take that approach in the wired world, they're going to find themselves thoughtfully planning how they'll spend their retirement.

Traditional strategic planning, rife with three-ring binders and 6 months of research, doesn't work in times of great change because it is too slow. Public relations plans used to be 6 inches thick, weigh 8 pounds, and project 3 to 5 years out. Today, that would be a ludicrous approach. Plans are revised weekly, often daily.

Today's successful companies put communications strategy center stage.

This is a change that started subtly within the last 10 years. The need for speed began, like most trends, at a very grassroots level, primarily by teenagers and particularly college students, who grew used to the hyper-speed connections available at most universities.

But even outside of the rarified atmosphere of the collegiate world, in the homes that relied on relatively slow dial-up connections, the Internet became the fastest mass medium by household penetration rate in history. It was instant, a communication tool that allowed bright young minds to do three things at once.

It's not uncommon to see a teenager sitting at the computer, communicating with friends online while listening to music and watching television. That's the way they grew up, and they're very comfortable with processing information at that pace.

All of this has led to the birth of a notion known as *Internet time*, a euphemism for change that happens at a pace that guardians of the traditional standards of society find astonishing. Internet time is something that most of today's senior business executives in the traditional world have not yet experienced. As a result, many who dismissed the Internet as a fad, or perhaps didn't notice it at all, are now scrambling to catch up. They're just starting to realize that the Internet is not CB radio. This is a permanent part of the cultural and business landscape.

Because public relations requires an ear to the ground, close contact with tastemakers, and a deep appreciation for society's trends, it is one of the first industries to adapt to this new world, and it now leads the way. The leaders of the public relations industry understand that the need to make an immediate impact in a cost-effective manner is of the highest priority in a world that moves on Internet time, where everything is compressed and attention spans are limited. Agility was something that the twenty-somethings who founded most of the dot coms now dominating the landscape instinctively realized and, today, agility is being adopted by smart companies, large and small.

ACCESS TO TOP DECISION MAKERS

Public relations professionals have access to the CEO as never before. Smart PR practitioners insist on it. That's a big switch. Why is this happening? Well, there is a new reality, which CEOs now understand. Public relations consistently plays a greater role in branding their companies, and their products, than any other communications tool, including advertising. The simple fact is that the top PR firms in this space have a stronger understanding of how value is articulated than an old-fashioned ad shop. And because the CEOs sometimes need to gain a greater understanding of the new rules and lexicon of Internet business, their dependence on public relations advisers becomes enormous. Just as the typical Internet business plan is rarely without an ample sprinkling of market size forecasts from Internet research firms, such as Jupiter and Forrester, it is also rarely completed without a heavy hand of influence from public relations advisors. The result is that public relations advisors have tremendous influence, counseling on greater business decisions than ever before. Now, public relations practitioners are often advising lawyers in many situations, such as initial public offerings (IPOs) and crisis communications, and counseling the CEOs on what they have to do to be successful. Today, the boardroom is calling the communications counselor.

PR INTERACTS IN NEW WAYS WITH NEW AUDIENCES

Public relations deals with the constituencies that matter most to a rapidly changing business. Apart from the media, the public relations world provides influence in circles involving industry analysts, venture capitalists, individual investors, and the financial community. These audiences are the foundation for building awareness and credibility among the Internet business "digerati" and for accomplishing important business objectives, such as customer loyalty and employee retention.

These new audiences demand to be a part of and, at times, guide the communications cycle—not merely act as recipients of corporate news and official statements. Communicators must reach out to these audiences online and off, develop interactive relationships with all constituencies, and embrace honest, responsive, and informal communications practices. (See Table 1-1.)

Yes, it is still called public relations—but it is much more than a mere conduit to the media. Public relations helps clients grow their businesses and improve their bottom lines. We do strategic counseling, special projects, research, press conferences, seminars, and create networking and partnering relationships.

This change hasn't been gradual. It's arrived at Internet speed, warping and woofing the nature of business relationships with the media as quickly as it has affected society in general.

NEW ERA OF BRANDING

Successful Internet branding is based on a shared belief that technology is aspirational and represents education, a feeling of

Table 1-1   New Ways of Interacting with New Audiences

YESTERDAY	TODAY
1. One-way communications –	1. Audience-driven communications cyclical
2. Local or regional communications	2. Instantly global audience
3. Planned news cycle	3. Rapid response news cycle
4. Preplanned press conference, mass-media release	4. Strategic exclusives, online press conference to support news media postexclusive
5. Media-driven communications strategy	5. Multiple constituencies of critical importance
6. Centralized control of news	6. Create news evangelists and viral campaigns to spread the word
7. One- to three-year plans	7. One- to three-month plans
8. Long research cycle	8. Quick snapshots and adaptive research cycle
9. Flacks	9. Business communications architects
10. Precedents, hard rules, and manuals drive the way you work	10. Entrepreneurial, fast strategy, and implementation will get you everywhere!

youth and coolness, and a path to enhanced status. The new reality that CEOs now understand is that the new era of branding demands greater context, an abundance of information, and great adherence to the evolution of Internet business. Branding today is often better communicated through demonstrating market demand and clear competitive differentiation than with flashy, clever graphics and hip, smart one-liners. The simple fact is that public relations firms in this period have a better opportunity to implement this new breed of branding and positioning and how value is articulated than traditional ad agencies.

Originally, the emerging brands of the Internet, the dot coms whose very reason for existence has been fueled by the medium's rise, immediately understood the tremendous change that was happening. Now that change continues to evolve by the traditional companies moving into the digital space big-time. That audience is less familiar with the old way of doing things, and is moving much more quickly. That's, in part, because they have different challenges. The challenge for a very traditional brand is to create *cachet*, an emotional change that needs to happen in their perception for employees, the media, and the public.

For both dot coms and reemerging enterprises, public relations is about creating integrity and credibility in a brand. A June 1999 survey by M Booth & Associates, a research firm, asked brand managers about how they worked. The study, based on responses of more than 100 brand managers, provides new evidence that public relations is the most effective way to establish brand credibility, to surround a brand in a particular editorial context, and provides the best return for the marketing dollar spent.

The majority of brand managers polled—51 percent—believe that public relations, when compared to advertising, sales promotion, and new media, is critical ("very important") for establishing brand credibility. In comparison, 44 percent characterized advertising as "very important," 21 percent said sales promotion, and 17 percent reported new media. Public relations also led the way as the most effective marketing communications discipline when editorial context is important. Fifty-one percent of brand managers said public relations was "very important" in targeting editorial context; 30 percent said advertising was "very important," 15 percent said sales promotion, and 14 percent picked new media.

Furthermore, brand managers felt that public relations is the best way to garner third-party endorsement: 39 percent said public relations was "very important," compared to 17 percent for advertising, 13 percent for sales promotion, and 10 percent for new media. Many fast movers understand this. And gradually, the rest of the world is catching on to the notion.

PUBLIC RELATIONS = INTERNET CURRENCY

Recently, the CEO of an online travel site left to become CEO of an incubated appliance shopping site. During her interview for the job, she told them that she would have two main budgetary priorities: one for human resources, the other for public relations. The venture capitalists behind the new company hired her on the spot. Venture capitalists, along with many business builders, now consider public relations activity when reviewing business plans, even if those plans are on a cocktail napkin devised on a San Francisco to New York redeye flight. Now, when a company approaches venture capitalists and present their business plan, the venture capitalist asks, "Who's doing your public relations?" If they don't know the firm, forget it. They will even suggest a firm to handle it. The right public relations firm is, in effect, a validation of a sound business plan.

So, in effect, public relations is now currency. A sound partnership with public relations counsel is validation of a sound business plan. Retaining public relations counsel indicates the company has an understanding of the marketplace; a well-planned, quickly executable communications strategy; and the ability to turn on the head of a dime. At a 1997 Silicon Alley Breakfast Club retreat at a Westchester County Country Club, Silicon Alley executives were grouped together at random and asked to devise a new business plan. The one common thread that ran through each plan was that public relations was the first step each group would take if they were to launch their fictitious businesses. To be clear, public relations has proven its role as a criteria for success in an arena where success is far from guaranteed.

It wasn't easy for business to adopt to this new paradigm.

Companies used to ask, "If I spend $5 million on my marketing campaign, how much am I going to get back in revenue?" They had an equation and could come up with a very easy metric—that $1 in marketing expensed equaled $5 in revenue.

Today, when a company asks that question, it has to redefine its definition of return. There is no longer just a return-on-investment (ROI) equation, at least by traditional standards.

ROI now means the cost of customer acquisition balanced against the spending and profitability of that customer. A company's corporate investment in public relations buys it customer loyalty, awareness, and positive buzz, which sometimes results in deferred revenue coming down the line. That's the founding principle of most Internet philosophy. Early on this was not irrational thinking. But as more copy cat dot coms started, operations flush with cash from the VC's sound business practices got out of hand. In April of 2000 the absurdity of business economics practiced by many of the dot coms were exposed. The Gartner Group, and Internet research firm, predicts that two-thirds of all e-commerce web sites will be out of business by 2002.

Amazon says their cost of customer acquisition is $16 per customer. The online trading companies claim their cost can exceed $250 per customer. That has nothing to do with revenue. Most of these companies are in the red or just teetering over the black. They're not measuring their return in any rational way, but playing as though the Internet were a land grab.

A report from Banc of America Securities sums up the dot-com debacle:

> The game many dot coms were pursuing was a fairly simple one. Spend the majority of your ad budgets on offline media and portal deals to drive brand awareness while simultaneously driving site traffic by acquiring click-through rates as cheaply as possible by buying "low end" commodity online media on the cheap. This methodology helped drive exposure to consumers (and even more important, investors), while at the same time boosting web site traffic, which was being utilized as a primary measure of valuation by the broader investment community. We believe this game is over.

So how do dot coms start a fresh game from here?

The traditional brands, the established brick and mortar and industrial age giants of the noncyber world, are starting to get that point.

They are actually beginning to put their marketing dollars in the right slots in order to successfully penetrate the emerging online community. But the actual tactics and strategies of executing a successful public relations campaign in the wired world is something many traditional businesses are still not able to do for themselves.

Public relations, in the past, always had a problem: you could never measure it. A CEO would say, "That's great. That's our new story. But what's it mean to our bottom line?" And the public relations person could only point to the number of stories generated, which can appear somewhat nebulous to certain chief executives.

Well, now you can measure what a story means to a bottom line, thanks to the Internet. When something appears in a newspaper or magazine, it spikes the web site.

The effect is particularly pronounced with electronic media.

When a CEO appears on CNBC, 10 seconds later the company's web site gets hit with a tremendous volume of use, allowing some measure of the impact. From past experience, the impact nearly always exceeds expectations.

Thus, it was no surprise that, when the dot-com companies in the early stages of the commercial Internet completed their first financing round, they often used the proceeds to pay their employees first, the rent second, and the public relations agency third. They knew that rising above the noise was a strategic part of their business development. That realization has led to a partnership that has helped create billion-dollar brands and celebrities.

What they realized was simple, but required a shift in thinking.

In the 1940s and 1950s there was a great middleweight fighter named Sugar Ray Robinson. He was called the best fighter in the world, pound for pound.

Well, dollar for dollar, there is no marketing tool better than public relations. In an age where things are moving faster than ever, the ability to shape your public image has never been greater.

Think not? Just remember the Christmas of 1999. It was heralded as the season when e-commerce would finally come into its own, taking substantial chunks out of the bricks and mortar marketplace. Eager to ride that wave, many companies went for broke. They spent millions of dollars on advertising. The result? A dismal failure, as consumers were overwhelmed by an endless flood of messages, and were quickly turned off.

But one happy result emerged from that. Many companies realized that they didn't have to spend $20 million, $15 million, or even $10 million a year to make a substantial impact on the market. No, they could spend a lot less than, say, $500,000, on public relations, and come away with results that would far outdistance the advertising.

The only way public relations can generate successful results is when a strong partnership exists between the public relations counselor and the client. When an agency is considering a potential client, there are several key questions to consider (see Table 1-2). First, who is their venture capital firm? The perception of your client will be shaped by who is backing them. A large venture capital firm like Hummer Winblad or Benchmark stepping up to the plate is much more imposing than a smaller firm. It sends a message to news outlets and others that the firm is being taken seriously at the highest levels.

Second, consider what round of funding the client is in and how much they have already raised.

Today, if a company doesn't have a recognizable venture capitalist and doesn't have a minimum of $15 million to $20 million in the second round, most reputable public relations agencies would probably pass on accepting them as a client.

Again, it's a matter of perception. A prominent venture-capital firm investing large amounts of money gives added weight to the company's profile, underlining the seriousness with which their business concept is regarded. The public relations firm needs evidence to convince an increasingly skeptical news media that a client is important. Nothing says that as much as a large war chest funded by prominent investors. And, as mentioned before, cutting through the clutter is a very expensive game. If a firm is undercapitalized, it will not have the resources to do what it takes.

The alliance evaluation game between business and public relations firms works the other way as well, by the way. Venture capitalists want to know the public relations firms of the companies they fund. Gradually, the rest of the world is catching on to the notion that public relations has become a form of cur-

Table 1-2   Prospective Client Checklist: A Guide for Every Public Relations Counselor

YES	NO	QUESTION
☐	☐	1. Does the client have a sustainable business model?
☐	☐	2. Can the client articulate clearly its definition of success in 3 months? In 6 months? In 1 year?
☐	☐	3. Does the client have adequate funding to support aggressive business growth for the foreseeable future?
☐	☐	4. Does the client have other mission-critical communications systems in place, such as customer service, sales, and marketing?
☐	☐	5. Does the client have a solid management team in place that can respond to changing market pressures quickly and intelligently?
☐	☐	6. Does the client demonstrate a commitment to public relations, verbally and in previous actions?
☐	☐	7. Can the client make executive business decisions and act upon them quickly?
☐	☐	8. Has the client established notable business partner relationships to accelerate its acquisition of customers?
☐	☐	9. Has the client established solid technology partnerships to build and maintain superior technology solutions?
☐	☐	10. Do you believe the client intends to build a long-term relationship with you built on mutual respect?

rency, a way to get the maximum bang for your buck. Venture capitalists now review proposed public relations activity when they analyze business plans, whether those plans are on a cocktail napkin or in a three-ring binder.

A third factor that needs to be considered by the public relations agency when reviewing a potential account is the newsworthiness of a client. It is important for an agency to believe that a client has publicity potential, for public relations can only be as effective as the business models, plans, operations, and, most importantly, people it represents.

If there are doubts about whether the client can truly cut through the Internet clutter, a professional agency should not take on the client.

A fourth point to use in evaluating a potential client is the company's ability to react. Both parties in a public relations pact have to be able to move quickly. If the potential client can't move fast, if it's overly cautious and bound up in bureacracy and process, then the agency can't be successful. And every agency wants clients that make them look good.

An agency should also have a sense of the client's level of commitment. You should have a feeling that management knows how to build an organization quickly and that they are committed to public relations.

For example, there was a company that was launching a new employee-focused portal. Built into their business model was a significant and inherent privacy issue that would, at the very least, ruffle the feathers of the online privacy experts whose opinion is paramount.

This company, however, did not understand that there was a privacy issue, and refused to acknowledge and deal with it. This kind of reaction is indicative of a poor level of commitment and understanding of their marketplace.

The increased status currently enjoyed by some public relations firms also has its drawbacks. It can sometimes create a false feeling of invulnerability, which, in turn, can lead to recklessness if not checked. That's why it's vitally important for public relations professionals to maintain their sense of integrity. Credibility is everything when individuals are trying to decide what to believe in the information assault, established brand names have earned that credibility many times over, and public relations professionals are the intermediary between readers and that credibility.

Today, the marketplace *depends* upon credibility. The snake-oil salespeople, the "flacks" of yesteryear, have either hit the high road or been left in the dust. Public relations professionals who understand that and don't lose respect for the impact and value of journalism over the needs of their clients will be the clear winners because that's where public relations can make the difference.

It is more important than ever to reach the journalist on a personal level, get them interested and aware of what's going on, and convey the truth to them so they can do their story and people can read it. That's as difficult for journalists as it is for the consumer, exponentially increasing the importance of the trusted intermediaries.

Since its first release in 1994, the Middleberg/Ross Media in Cyberspace study has annually tracked the latest developments related to journalists' use of cyberspace, including the growth of online publishing, techniques used in developing stories, and how reporters work with sources online. The study also explores such topical issues as reporting of online rumors and the use of wireless devices and instant messaging.

The most recent edition was released in March 2000, the sixth annual study. The survey was sent to more than 4000 magazine and newspaper editors throughout the country. The response rate was approximately 10 percent.

Nonresponse bias was minimized by comparing the sample of those who did respond with over 3000 responses from previous years and by making more than 90 follow-up phone calls.

What the sixth edition of the study found was crucial to understanding how the Internet is being used now, and how it might be used in the future.

The survey showed that, as expected, the overall use of the Internet by journalists was growing significantly. They used it for article research, development of story ideas and sources, and for communicating with readers.

But the big news was that a majority of journalists said they found most web sites lacking in credibility. At the same time, they said they would, with additional confirmation, consider reporting Internet rumors and using information found on the Internet for stories.

That's a significant finding. It shows that, despite reservations, the Internet is too good a tool to be ignored by the journalists. Nearly three-fourths of respondents said they go online daily, a huge jump from 1999's 48 percent. E-mail has also become more popular for communication with known sources as well as readers. New technologies are also jumping, with instant messaging extremely popular with one-quarter of the respondents.

There's no turning back from that trend. The study confirmed in stark detail how the Internet has become woven into the fabric of modern journalism. Journalists are playing by new rules—developing story ideas online, reporting online rumors, and going to corporate and association web sites for information, especially when a story breaks.

The conclusion one reaches from that is that public relations professionals who understand and take advantage of these new trends, without losing respect for the impact and value of journalism, will be the clear winners.

Professor Ross, perhaps echoing the thoughts of journalism professors and professionals, found the overall trends of the survey troubling, particularly with regard to credibility. While hailing the rising use of the Internet, he also noted that questionable ethical practices were also expanding.

"Media web sites freely link to advertisers and to previously published articles, often failing to credit other publications' work," Ross said. "Many respondents also admitted to publishing rumors, often with little or no substantiation, and to using online sources whose credibility had not been adequately established."

Ross was right to question where everything is headed. Because in the answers to the survey's questions, journalists seemed to indicate that faster and looser was the trend in reporting.

When journalists responding to the survey were asked to rank web site credibility, the only sites that were found to have a high degree of credibility were trade associations' sites. Message board and chat groups were seen as least credible.

Still, lack of credibility in message boards and chat groups would not keep most journalists from using web postings, especially if the information were confirmed elsewhere. Seventeen percent said they would consider doing so in the future, even if not confirmed elsewhere, a highly troubling percentage. That means nearly one in five reporters would use information they did not trust if it suited their purposes. That's a grave threat to credibility.

The trend continued in even more alarming fashion. When it comes to reporting rumors, 60 percent of respondents said they would consider reporting an Internet rumor if confirmed by an independent source, while only 12 percent said they would not, and 3 percent admitted to already having done so. Nineteen percent said they would report the rumor if it came from a "reliable" professional news site.

Taken in its best light, what all of this points out is that the Internet has expanded the scope of where journalists obtain their information. That makes the job of public relations as a focused and reliable source ever more important. The public relations professional has an equal stake in the credibility of stories that appear in publications.

Because the survey underlines the point that almost any source of information on the Internet will be considered by harried journalists under pressure to deliver stories, they need to be able to trust their intermediaries. Public relations professionals with solid reputations and great contacts will stand an even greater chance of being able to position their clients in the news.

The expansion in news outlets points out another interesting trend. Public relations people who understand the wired world often find themselves reaching out to influencers that aren't necessarily part of the mainstream. A case in point is Harry Knowles.

Harry, if you don't know him, started a site called "Ain't It Cool News" out of his bedroom in Austin, Texas. A true movie fan, he tapped into the large number of people who loved to gossip about movies, forming a community where the people who saw early previews of upcoming movies or were involved in making them could talk about what they had seen and give their opinions.

Even though it was run out of a bedroom, it quickly became just as important for a public relations agency to reach out to Harry Knowles as to *Variety* or any other entertainment publication. Despite the vast difference in their financials, both Harry Knowles and *Variety* have influence over a large and important segment of the community that public relations firms are trying to reach.

In the wired age, influencers now come in all shapes and forms. There are a number of very influential e-mail lists that shape how the media—and the people the media go to for quotes—think about certain things.

One important example is the Pho list, named after a Vietnamese soup dish eaten at informal gatherings of this music-/technology-centric group at weekly meetings around the world. Pho list members include record industry executives, journalists, technology company personnel, music publishers, and industries related to technology.

Both online and in the real world, Pho is a place where ideas are bred, concepts hatched, and perceptions shaped. In short, it's a place public relations people need to monitor as it's a breeding ground for the stories that will emerge in the mainstream media.

Lists like Pho are heavily influencing how the rest of the world thinks about issues like privacy and digital security, shaping what's cool and what's not. They sway reporters who are looking for context and validity for their own beliefs.

What these lists do is talk about issues, and not just whether a company is going to do well, but the meatier issues, the ones that need more context, the areas that challenge everyone who needs to understand and make critical decisions based on what's going on.

This emerging new world of communications in the Internet economy is one that has many corporate hearts filled with dread. It has also left many entrepreneurs without direction as to how the Internet has changed the role of public relations. To accelerate the transition from yesterday's enterprise to tomorrow's Internet worked organization, a new breed of public relations practitioner has arrived, one that blends traditional public relations with online communications to create proactive, integrated, and groundbreaking campaigns for clients—the e-communicator. Vice presidents of marketing and chief corporate communicators, as well as agency types and small business owners, know the suc-

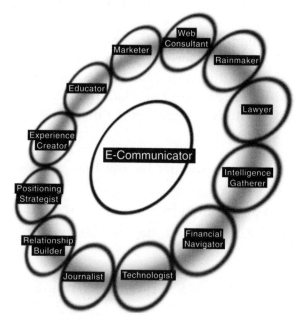

The New E-Communicator

Figure 1-1

cess of their companies and their personal careers depends on learning the new rules of the road. Whether you are a new recruit to the field of public relations, an entrepreneur managing all aspects of your business, or a life-long practitioner of media relations, you will need to understand that the old ways of doing business in this field are dead and a new set of e-communication rules exists. (See Figure 1-1.)

Many soon-to-be e-communicators are still uncomfortable with the Internet. Like Mr. Jones in that classic Bob Dylan song, they understand something is going on, but they don't understand what *it* is all about. They kind of get a feeling that they ought to do something, but they don't know what or how.

And the only way you, as an executive who understands *it*, are going to get through to them is to shake them by the lapels.

That's right. Get up and grab your boss firmly, and say: Gordon Gekko is dead! This is a whole new world, a whole new way of doing business. It's not your father's public relations world.

It's public relations in the wired world. A whole new ball-game. And anyone who wants to win in the digital world better have great public relations.

After you've apologized to your boss for shaking him or her by the lapels, you can do one more thing: calm down.

It's risky to play the Internet game, but it's also a tool that will increase productivity, ease communications, and effectively help get the message out at crunch and crisis time.

Just look at the facts:

- Seven people log on to the Internet for the first time every second
- There are more than 150 million Internet users worldwide
- The Internet growth rate is now faster outside the United States than inside

In 2 years there will be 350 million Internet users and 1 billion within this decade.

The reasons for public relations success can be broken out in several ways. But the overarching reason public relations has triumphed is really very simple. Today, in a world all but overwhelmed with information, public relations cuts through the B.S. to provide facts, facts people can make clear decisions on.

It appears in all mediums and conceivably at all times. It entertains, it enchants, and it doesn't require a break in concentration. It's the perfect medium—and it's the perfect communications technique for the perfect medium to deliver the perfect message.

Al Ries is considered one of the originators of today's thinking about the terms "branding" and "positioning." In his 1998 book, coauthored by his daughter Laura, entitled *The 22 Immutable Laws of Branding*, wrote,

"The birth of a brand is usually accomplished with publicity, not advertising." This from an ad guy.

That's a huge victory for public relations. But the war continues, and it promises to be a grueling campaign over the next few years. You need the strategies that will help you win that war.

THE FOUR FAST RULES OF COMMUNICATING IN THE DIGITAL AGE

Today, if businesses are not already in the digital arena, they probably have serious plans to get there.

Medical practices, law firms, accounting firms, and virtually every other type of business are reinventing themselves into dot-com companies. Industries as traditional as aluminum manufacturers and produce distributors have joined the revolution.

In order to better understand what's facing public relations people in the wired world, let's take a look at some of the changes facing certain companies and how these changes are upending business methodology as we know it.

A prime example of the massive change under way in the business world is the transformation of General Motors (GM), once the quintessential example of rust belt America and the epitome of the industrial age, into a truly wired company.

Instead of relying on the tried-and-true methods of its legendary chairman Alfred P. Sloan—clearly organized brands within a tightly integrated structure—GM has now become a bit of a maverick, driving the transformation of the auto industry onto the web by breaking down its old, inflexible ways of doing business and experimenting with new, fast-moving alliances.

By doing so, the company once again resembles the company that took several automobile companies and merged them together into what became General Motors.

Yes, recent changes have been gradual for the company when measured in real-world time. But, by GM standards, the company is moving at Internet speed.

By the last years of the twentieth century, GM reigned as the top car company in the world and the bulwark of the U.S. economy. But its business practices were clearly rooted in a world where careful planning and caution were the hallmarks of financial success.

Located in an antiquated 1950s downtown Detroit office building, the company looked old, smelled old, and acted old. Its processes were rooted in turn-of-the-century methodologies and careful planning, all controlled by a hierarchical system that emphasized a steady, formal procedure to enact virtually every business practice.

In 1996, for example, the company estimated that it took approximately 4 years to complete each new car-development cycle.

Like many companies in the 1990s, General Motors was astonished to see the incredible changes wrought by the introduction of the Internet into standard business procedure. Realizing that its future was riding on its ability to adapt to changing times and an emerging world marketplace, GM began a gradual transformation.

While it was not the first company to move into the Internet world, when it did make its move, it did so with authority.

Today, the company has introduced several new alliances with car companies around the world and various new Internet divisions that have helped them shed their slow-moving image. They are now seen as a formidable presence in the online automotive marketplace.

In perhaps its most important move to embrace consumer passion for the Internet, the company now has a very impressive consumer-oriented web site, GMBuyPower.com, which offers customers ways to customize auto preferences and locate dealers.

Restricted by franchise laws from selling directly to consumers, GM has nonetheless effectively harnessed the power of the Internet to drill down in specific categories. The company now allows consumers to preview their automobile choices online and walk in to dealerships armed with an impressive array of knowledge. That has translated into not only increased consumer awareness but also, in many instances, increased sales of GM products.

The business side has also seen improvements. Business customers can now log on to GMSupplyPower.com (see Figure 2-1) to access production schedules, buy and sell excess inventory, and obtain manufacturing information.

Even more impressively, the company has entered into partnerships to create an automotive exchange that will allow dealers to inform each other about what's available on each lot. The company has also launched an OnStar-enabled vehicle partnership, which allows franchises to implement new programs that use the directional navigation device.

Finally, in what may be the ultimate realization of supply-and-demand change created by the Internet, the company has indicated that it hopes to build the majority of its cars in the near future based on specific orders from customers.

While that change requires massive internal restructuring and integrating of the entire car-buying and manufacturing

Figure 2-1

process, it is a step toward eliminating excess inventory and controlling costs, a potentially huge savings on high-ticket items like cars and car parts.

Like some its traditional competitors and leaders in big business, the company has formed a separate unit, e-GM, to accelerate the integration and introduction of Internet services to the marketplace.

Companies attempting to transform a historic brand into one that moves swiftly, respond to customer needs, and take the lead in the Internet business economy find that the point person assigned to implement the changes faces a painful, often resented task. Table 2-1 outlines some of the challenges these traditional businesses face on the communications front.

Many times, these challenges must be undertaken by *intrapreneurs*, or employees of a company who have an entrepreneurial streak. These intrapreneurs are often maverick executives who are either brought in to a company as a catalyst for change or long-time employees who have enough vision to resist the ties to the old methods and the willingness to pull their organization kicking and screaming into tomorrow's business world.

These executives face unique brand and communications challenges. But because large firms are well financed and have a base of operations established, the changes can often be affected rather swiftly once a decision is made to move forward.

In fact, many companies are so excited about embracing the potential of the Internet, they've resorted to taking their best employees and putting them in the dot-com division, often with the idea that these units will go public, thereby enriching the parent company and key employees.

Large companies like GM, IBM, United Airlines, and other well-known names in traditional industry already dominate or are near the top of their specific market niches.

Yet it is still possible to build a brand in categories that are somewhat saturated on the Internet and in the real world.

Today, there are more businesses than ever before entering the Internet space to meet market demands that did not exist even a few years ago or have plans based on untested concepts.

Table 2-1   Communication Challenges of Traditional Enterprises

Siloism: Because many Internet business initiatives cut across several product areas, creating a coordinated communications strategy can be sticky.

Speaking to new audiences: Many larger businesses are now packaging services and products targeted to Internet start-ups and emerging businesses, which creates a love/hate dichotomy for the traditional brands.

The "I don't handle that" syndrome: Roles in traditional communications departments are specialized and focused, presenting an obstacle to integrated offline/online public relations and marketing.

Speed: Layers of approval and going before "news release boards" can slow the announcement of news significantly.

CEO as spokesperson: One CEO representing several areas of business does not guarantee all Internet business initiatives will get top attention in the media.

Some excellent offerings have been introduced without the supportive benefit of consumer-driven market development to online access to initial public stock offerings.

It is sometimes easy to spot a product or service that seemingly has no chance of succeeding, but somehow receives a surprising amount of financial support for no understandable reason.

Often—or, at least often enough until the famous dot-com crash during the first quarter of 2000—investors would fall in love with the management team or simply throw up their hands and say, "I don't understand it, but it sounds good. I'll give you $5 million."

That led, of course, to a situation where some very questionable online businesses were being launched, money-eating machines that didn't have a prayer, even if they were well financed. The dot-com crash underscored just how many of these businesses were not based on reality, but on speculation.

Surprisingly, there are still such businesses being launched every day by people who think they have to get in on the gold rush. Unfortunately, besides being sure-fire losers for their own investors, these businesses make it tougher for sustainable, credible businesses to emerge on the Internet business landscape.

*   *   *

New companies face incredibly tough communications barriers to entry in the dot-com horizon. To better understand and appreciate what it takes to make it in the dot-com world, let's take a look at some of the monstrous issues confronting these companies.

The first huge barrier is *legitimization*. This means that a company entering a marketplace must compete like one of the established market leaders in order to be taken seriously.

Next comes demonstrating *sustainability*. The challenge for companies entering a new world is to show that they're more than just another "me too" business. How do you convince your potential customers that you're not a flash in the pan, but will be around to service their needs if they choose to form a relationship with you?

Education is the third step in the process. If no one understands your business or the category you're in, how will you convince him or her to invest, purchase from, or otherwise interact with your company? You must educate the market immediately as to the nature of your business.

Finally, a new business must project *leadership* on the key issues of responsibility in the Internet space: privacy, security, and customer care. They are the Holy Trinity of anyone entering a new world, but particularly resonate in the wired world.

Advertising.com is a great example of a business that entered into its space with a bang. The company relaunched its business with a new corporate identity in January 2000. The online advertising sector was already dominated by major companies such as CMGI and DoubleClick. Through increased marketing, rapid consolidation, and buyouts of smaller competitors, each of these large companies was racing to become the biggest fish in the sea. Advertising.com executives did not want to play that game. They wanted to make sure the public would regard them with the same esteem as the two market leaders.

To achieve that, Advertising.com began behaving like it was already a market leader, and used a savvy sense of public relations to emphasize its differences with its competitors. The company, which started out with the name TeknoSurf.com, immediately made an important move by obtaining the powerful URL Advertising.com. Although the price was never revealed, anyone with an ounce of Internet sense realized that a URL so significant to the industry most likely came at a steep price. This immediately showed they were serious players.

The newly christened Advertising.com then set out to target three specific areas where it knew it could beat the competition. First, the Advertising.com technology, an online advertising algorithm, enabled the optimization and ability to serve ads to the web, e-mail, and the desktop. This was unique to Advertising.com and made them stand out from even the big players. Second, CostPerClick/Performance-based pricing, was a relatively nascent idea that had not been widely used at the time. Advertising.com took a risk to implement this strategy with their proprietary technology, which, in the end, paid off. Finally, company growth was a fact that was well worth publicizing—revenues had grown 230 percent in 3 months and the staff had grown from 6 employees in February 1999 to over 100 in January 2000.

In the latter category, Advertising.com was one of a handful of established Internet businesses based in Baltimore, Maryland. Not a big story hook, but an interesting enough peg to create some editorial opportunities that might not have otherwise happened. The company also touted its solid, young management team, including brothers Scott and John Ferber, who were awarded the "Entrepreneur of the Year" award from accounting giant Ernst & Young. Thus positioned as a company based in an Internet outpost and run by a very smart entrepreneurial team, Advertising.com then began to tell the story of why its product was better than the rest.

Since one of the chief issues in the sector at that time was privacy, Advertising.com emerged with a strict privacy standard that challenged the somewhat squishy standards of their competitors. It was a bold move, but one that gave them instant credibility and recognition within the advertising and Internet communities. It also served notice that this was a company that intended to chart its own course, rather than be yet another tasty company that could be gobbled by CMGI and DoubleClick.

Figure 2-2

These tactics established Advertising.com as an innovative company determined to be in the game for some time. Their name was huge—an amazing, category-killer URL. They proved they were legitimate, would be able to sustain themselves for the foreseeable future, built awareness, and underlined their credibility among key audiences. This helped them break through the clutter of the "startup stampede," something very few companies have been able to achieve in the crowded market, particularly when matched against entrenched competitors. (See Figure 2-2.)

CareerExperience.com is another example of a company that managed to put some distance between itself and powerful competitors. Imagine the number of online services offering career counseling, and you'll realize the daunting task facing CareerExperience.com as it entered the career resource and development marketplace. It truly faced a saturated field. But at the time of its launch, the company had several unique slants on its definition of career resource and found unique ways to highlight these. CareerExperience.com sponsored an ongoing contest that allowed a winner to experience his or her dream job for a day. The first winner was a guy who wanted to be a professional golfer. He not only received a new set of clubs but also an invitation to the Pro-AM with Vijay Singh before the Buick Rye Classic at the prestigious Rye, New York, Country Club.

Capitalizing on the attention surrounding the tournament, CareerExperience.com used the occasion to present the *Today* show host Matt Lauer with a Scotty Cameron putter used by Tiger Woods. These high-profile events not only brought national, immediate awareness to the company but also helped highlight that the site was the largest source of sports careers. When users clicked on, the site offered much more than contests. It also allowed visitors to read first-person narratives about what it would be like to experience various careers. Want to be a multimedia producer? You could read about what it was like to have that job, and the site even offered a producer who could answer your questions. In addition, guidance and training resources provided actionable steps for obtaining that ideal job. Site traffic spiked by 60,000 the morning following the contest, allowing them to grab brand awareness and the public's attention right out of the gate. That's almost a necessity in that field, and it allowed CareerExperience.com to gain traction upon which to build a solid communications program in a challenging market.

While startups, by necessity, have to reach out to new sets of customers, established brands are also recognizing the need to reach audiences never before envisioned before the Internet.

IBM is one particular example. By now, it's become business legend how IBM missed the boat in the early days of computing, betting big on mainframes over desktops. It was the textbook example of corporate intransigence in the face of market challenges.

But IBM has lately been among the innovators in its field. As we write this, the company is making a strong push into assisting startup Internet firms, offering various levels of assistance in hardware and software that are designed to create a new market for the company's goods and services.

As a result, IBM is now considered among those few enterprises able to transform themselves to attract and develop relationships with an entirely new audience, something forecasters in the early 1980s couldn't have envisioned.

Another example of a traditional brand reaching out via the Internet to embrace a new market is Ford Motor Company. Like General Motors, Ford was a bedrock old-economy company, seemingly stuck in a muddy trench when it came to moving forward in the wired world.

Not any more. One of Ford's efforts has been to reach out to the teenage market—a market ripe with prospective customers—through sponsorship of Bolt.com.

Bolt.com, which offers content, community, and commerce, is one of the most popular teen sites on the Internet, targeting the 14- to 17-year-old audience, who are thinking and talking about driving, but may be years away from making their first car purchase.

But Ford is building early brand awareness by sponsoring a cars channel on Bolt.com that allows teens to talk about their driving experiences, upload pictures of their cars, and vote for the "cooler" car. The company has also begun placing advertisements that hit a cool, hip audience. It's changing its image from stodgy to sophisticated, and a customer that grows up with that impression is more likely to think kindly of Ford's cars when they first enter the market.

Perhaps the two most widely heralded attempts by old-image brands to unite with the dot-com world were the cases of American Express and Sony, two vastly different companies with the same objective: reach a technologically sophisticated audience that perceived them as old school.

American Express won its new audience by launching its Blue Card, targeted at an audience that needed to form a new image of the financial services company. American Express was perceived as for an older, wealthier, somewhat stuffier crowd, a financially secure group that could afford to pay off its purchases in full each month. (See Figure 2-3.)

The Blue Card represents the rethinking of what American Express has come to stand for. The card was launched alongside a big promotional concert in Central Park by recording artist Sheryl Crow, who also donated a guitar that was in the shape of a Blue Card to The Elizabeth Glaser Pediatric AIDS Foundation. Far after the last notes of the concert died, a new impression of American Express had been born—the company was now reaching out to a new element, one that represented the future rather than the establishment.

Similarly, Sony faced a market challenge from the rise of the Internet. Although the company was entrenched in such cool fields as consumer electronics and entertainment, it had not yet penetrated the emerging world of the Internet and computing. Thus was born the concept of the Vaio, a device that was targeted at the technologically sophisticated user with lots of disposable income.

Rather than sit back and watch its audience be gradually siphoned off by competitors, Sony took the bold step of making its computer a status symbol, a must have for the technology elite who had a big budget to play around with new electronic toys.

It's something you'll see more companies do in the coming years. And underlining that transformation will be the job of public relations professionals.

Audiences both embrace and reject what these companies stand for, requiring a trained intermediary in public relations to restore some sense of balance.

For example, American Express was the card people considered when they wanted a charge device that would symbolize their wealth. Yes, they said, an American Express card will show I've joined the club.

But the card also conveyed that possessing one made a consumer somewhat stuffy. That's a negative impression, one that can only be allayed by the proper positioning in the media of new images and a new storyline.

As companies enter new marketplaces, new terms keep cropping up to describe the markets they are not only joining but also creating.

The most common market on the Internet is business to consumer, sometimes known as B2C among the digerati. Its

Figure 2-3

concept is as old as commerce: a business is devised that will attempt to reach the public.

In the spring 2000, as the dot-com world experienced its first serious slowdown, a new terminology started to gain traction. Former B2C businesses began transforming themselves into B2B, or business-to-business, companies. The idea was that their goods and services could also help their fellow businesspeople to achieve their objectives.

The idea was really more a matter of clever positioning by many adopters of the term. Having experienced trouble penetrating the consumer market, many Internet companies attempted to keep their financial boat floating by painting themselves into a broad new market landscape filled with businesses eager to tap their services.

After the B2B fad became part of the landscape, new terms began emerging that carried the increasingly fragmenting e-commerce market into new territories.

X2X became a hybrid, hyped evolution of B2B and exchanges. The idea behind X2X was that it would connect seemingly disparate market segments with each other.

For example, if you were in grocery supply exchanges as a B2B business, and decided to enter the home appliance marketplace, you became an X2X business. In other words, you entered a market perceived as wholly unrelated to your present business, but were attempting to fill a new niche that didn't exist before.

Almost 600 such X2X exchanges quickly sprang up by the spring 2000, many of them former B2C businesses that had morphed into B2B and now were making yet another transition.

Another interesting emerging business trend was the P2P market, for peer-to-peer, or people-to-people businesses. This market relied on a network of personal contacts to work for each other in a newly created business environment. One particular example of this trend is Refer.com.

Spawned out of the famous Idealab Internet business incubator in Pasadena, California, Refer.com allowed people to refer their colleagues to available job positions by forwarding their resume to interested customers, in effect serving as employment headhunters. If the referral was successful, the person received a percentage of the employment referral fee, much as a professional job-search firm would.

For instance, if I know my friend Lisa is looking for a new job in decorating, and I see that a job listing is posted looking for an interior decorator, I can forward her on-file resume automatically through the site. One peer helping another.

Another interesting market segment emerging from the growing Internet marketplace is B2G, or business-to-government. This is a market poised to explode, as many local and state governments have been extremely slow to adopt to the wired world.

In this new form of connection, businesses help government organizations build their own internal infrastructures, provide services, and generally assist in the wiring of local and state offices. If you're facilitating the online filing of property taxes, or helping someone register a car by clicking a mouse, you're in the B2G game.

One other interesting phenomenon affecting the business climate in the summer 2000 was that companies were reconciling their online and offline businesses.

No longer was the dot-com world a separate division. The growing acceptance of the Internet as a mainstream medium and the way customers are responding to that medium have led many businesses to begin to fully integrate online operations into all their services.

Respected New York research firm Jupiter Communications said in the summer 2000 that bricks and clicks—as such reconciliations are referred to in Internet parlance—is the winning way to go. Jupiter reported some 68 percent of consumers research online and purchase offline, a figure that underlines the wisdom of streamlining corporate operations.

Of course, wanting to unify your company's various business divisions and actually achieving that are two different matters. There are a number of issues from the offline world that aren't so easily addressed in the online world.

One case in point is customer care. There are many brands that have excellent offline customer care, but have found that the technology required to achieve an equal measure of such service online is particularly hard to do. The level of staffing to provide real-time customer service is daunting in the 24/7 wired world, as many companies that had very little customer service experience in the real world learned when they ventured online.

The all-time classic customer-service snafu occurred when the Walt Disney Company left a relative handful of employees on duty for Christmas. While the company's CD-ROM of *The Lion King* proved vexing to customers, the busy signals they received from a customer-service center that was swamped with calls and had no personnel to stem the tide became the stuff of industry legend.

One prime example of the trend toward unification is, again, American Express. Besides their venture in attracting a new, technologically hip audience with the Blue Card, consumers could now get their reward program information online, obtain points for online activity, or review their bill online. Coupled with this was offline loyalty point redemption, online resources for offline purchasing, and offline point accumulation redeemable for online purchases. For American Express, bringing their various divisions into a united operation was a matter of expanding the business. For others, it was viewed as a matter of survival.

CVS was a massive drug chain that felt its business was being rapidly cannibalized by the proliferation of Internet operations in the health and beauty sector. The rise of Drugstore.com (the possible entry of the feared Internet titan Amazon.com into the market) and PlanetRX.com made CVS realize it had to get up to speed immediately. They felt that the new upstarts were so well funded that it would only be a matter of time before even their established brand was challenged.

Rather than build its own infrastructure, CVS bought Soma.com, a relative newcomer to the health and beauty world, but one that had a solid back-office system that could be adopted for use at CVS. The company has been integrating that operation into its own business, hoping to retain its retail customers and attract new ones on the Internet.

The wisdom of that decision remains to be seen. But the wisdom of two massive entertainment operations in the reconciliation of their online and offline businesses has—at least so far—proven to be a disaster.

Disney, which launched the Go Network, and Time Warner, which initially made its entry onto the Internet via Pathfinder, both learned that leveraging a traditional offline brand isn't a matter of cutting and pasting it into the Internet world.

In Disney's case, the company spent huge amounts of money trying to integrate the various arms of its empire into something called the Go Network, a term which meant little to consumers and, in fact, had a logo that was confused with the Idealab-incubated Goto.com. Disney did not attempt to leverage its own well-established and beloved brand names and intellectual property onto the Internet. Instead, they insisted that the Go Network would become its own brand. In fact, its intense legal corporate identity battles with Goto.com resulted in a victory for Goto and necessitated a rebranding effort for Disney's Go Network. (See Figure 2-4.) To date, the public has given the Go Network concept a resounding thumbs down.

Time Warner had a slightly different idea. It realized the value of its established brand names, and attempted to build a

Disney's Go.com Network

Goto.com

Figure 2-4

portal based around new brands that were relatively similar to the famous ones, but slightly different in content. The public didn't buy it. Instead of building a solid base with its assets, the company wound up diluting its traditional brands and creating a hub that never took off. The Pathfinder name was finally retired, one of the Internet's most infamous crash and burns.

The first step for a public relations professional who needs to support such dramatic changes is to create a level of product differentiation and devise a way to meet a market demand currently unfilled by other offerings.

In other words, stand out from the crowd.

Of course, that's easier for a business to accomplish if it has the money to buy the best big-name talent. Nothing separates a new company from the pack than having a Whoopi Goldberg or William Shatner to tout its services, as Flooz.com or Priceline do.

Of course, it also helps to have a good product. Some of you with a bit more gray hair may remember Piels beer. The Milwaukee beer company made a big splash in the late 1950s with its terrific advertisements featuring Burt and Harry Piels, two lovable, regular-guy cartoon character schlubs who loved Piels beer. Unfortunately, Piels is the perfect example of a great communications campaign in support of a bad product.

Piels was just an average beer back in the 1950s, fighting to eke out a market place between such giants as Budweiser and

Figure 2-5

Miller. (See Figure 2-5.) At the time, broadcast television and radio dominated the beer market, and Piels came up with an ingenious campaign featuring Burt and Harry. The commercials touched a nerve with the beer-drinking public and were an immediate hit. Beer sales climbed dramatically as a result.

But eventually sales leveled off and then began to drop. As that happened, Piels went back and did some consumer research, asking buyers what had caused the drop off in sales. The bad news for Piels was the customer response: loved the commercials, but the beer tasted awful.

Which proves a point: a beloved campaign with characters people can relate to are fine, but in the end it still boils down to the product and product's quality. No matter how good the public relations, no matter how good the advertising, your long-term sustainability won't happen without a product that has a clearly understood value proposition that people will come back to time and again. That's where it all starts. But even in a crowded marketplace, there's always room for someone who has a new twist, a new angle, and knows how to communicate and promote it.

There are four rules of communications applicable to all business. Following these rules may not ensure success, but in today's economy, ignoring them is a sure-fire recipe for failure.

The first rule is, simply, move fast. In the Internet economy, the element of speed, of moving fast and forward, has taken on a completely new dimension.

In public relations, speed is not just about getting news out the door. To public relations, speed is reflected in the way a company disseminates corporate information and industry intelligence, works with customers, and forms alliances with business partners.

True speed enables a company to work at the pace of its consumer and business audiences.

The perception of speed enables a company's external partners to help the company get to where it needs to go at a breakneck pace.

The essence of speed helps attract key talent, acquire venture capital, attract killer partners, and lure infrastructure services such as web architecture, legal and accounting services, and, of course, public relations.

A company that is entrenched in bureaucracy, taking months to get releases signed, exudes a low confidence factor in their ability to meet market promises. In short, slow companies, large and small, are perceived as dinosaurs that just don't get it. And no one will wait around for them to learn.

Speed is the weapon not only of the first movers in a category but also the ultimate secret of the category winners. The companies that can enter and grow within a market category by responding swiftly to market pressures and competitive intelligence are the ones that will succeed.

Amazon.com is the most oft-cited, recognizable example of a company that has embraced speed-to-market communications. Amazon has created and conducted groundbreaking campaigns, sometimes in spite of itself, many of which have resulted in positive spikes in its stock price.

The secret to the company's success in public relations has been speed, the ability to change plans on the fly, and the talent to make those plans understood by the public and investors.

The reason they're able to pull this off is CEO Jeff Bezos. It's no accident that Amazon has become so big. Bezos is a promotional genius in e-commerce success. A company really does reflect the personality and the tone of its leader, crucial in the fast-changing world of the Internet where business plans can turn on a dime. The key with Amazon is that Bezos really understands public relations, really gets what its tremendously critical role is in building his business.

Amazon has built a brand at Internet speed, and it's an adaptable brand as well. It has become the de facto search engine for consumers seeking books, music, household tools, drugs, and many other items perceived as necessary for an improved quality of life. More importantly, it's the company most people cite when they want to gauge the temperature of the Internet world.

One of the most clever public relations tactics Amazon has introduced is the dissemination of a press release announcing that there will soon be another press release issued to announce a new marketing initiative.

The strategy is brilliant, and while it may be a short-term success as other companies begin to flood reporters with Amazon-like announcements and a backlash occurs, it succeeded in building Amazon into one of the Internet's most recognizable brands.

These appetizer announcements work like this. Two days before the marketing results are to be released, Amazon builds a high level of anticipation, issuing a rather terse announcement that it will soon issue its results. In effect, Amazon is getting two bites of the apple on the same news, no mean feat in a saturated financial news sector.

That sort of thinking has to flow from the top down. You can tell that's the case just by watching Bezos maneuver his way through the minefields financial reporters try to lead him through. It's pretty amazing to watch him in action.

"Jeff, aren't you worried about losing all this money?"

"No."

"Why aren't you?"

"Because we can make a profit tomorrow by cutting our advertising and marketing budgets accordingly. But we're not going to do that."

This is a guy who is so firmly convinced he's on the right track that nothing will shake his confidence. That confidence translates in the media.

Even though analysts will talk about skepticism that the ultimate business plan will succeed, and question whether the company will survive, the stories that appear about Amazon.com rarely are disaster stories that firmly insist this company is going out of business.

Instead, the stories that appear indicate that Jeff Bezos doesn't care how much he loses, and if people are worried about their earnings, they are worried about the wrong thing. What he's done is shift attention away from something that could potentially hurt the company toward a forward-looking message. He gets that message across and people remember it.

The instinct to do that is something that's innate in an individual. That's why guys like Jeff Bezos are so rare. They have an innate second sense of what makes good copy, how to handle and massage media, and know how to deal with the crisis situations, all while working quickly. No one can say with any degree of certainty whether he's right or wrong. It's a question only time will answer.

Speed is crucial on the Internet.

When an idea is formed and a product is conceived, many organizations need to go out into the marketplace almost instantaneously, usually within a matter of weeks. There's no time to sit and dither about the right thing to do. The market simply will not wait.

It's not just the companies themselves that have had to adapt to the speed of the Internet. The various support functions of outside agencies—including legal, public relations, advertising, and marketing—also have had to change their tactics.

They have to move as fast as the entrepreneur, channeling their vision about the changing market into the same frame as their client and understanding instinctively how their client fits into the bigger picture. There simply isn't time for any other way.

Public relations has certainly had to learn how to think like the entrepreneurs it now represents. Before the Internet, public relations was more like advertising, in that it was dependent upon market research. Today most companies have to build both a brand and a company that can go public in 18 to 24 months.

To be highly successful in your communications strategy, it's a good idea to think like a kind of entrepreneur: the venture capitalist. That means a public relations person must understand and make judgments about a business model.

The first step in developing positioning, messaging, and communications strategy for a new brand is to assess whether this business is going to work against a defined set of criteria. Venture capitalists tend to develop rounded portfolios and don't keep all their eggs in one basket. Communications agencies should do the same.

Secondly, a communicator must represent his or her cause, issue, client, or organization to the journalist/analyst community in a way that's understandable and relevant.

Much of our job as public relations professionals is to take the language of the technologists and translate it into simple, common business language. That is not easy to do, but it is a talent that a public relations person needs. And all of this has to be done at breakneck speed.

Think about it: how do you take a company that has no identity, no awareness, no recognition for what makes them special, and build that into something so recognized and trustworthy that a consumer will hand over precious data and make a purchase? That is our mission.

Public relations can accomplish all those tasks and do it faster and better and cheaper than other forms of communications. One of its secrets is its close contact with the fastest means of mass communications, the media. Its other secret is its newfound embrace of the entrepreneurial style. In other words, go beyond the role of media conduit!

Adaptive branding is yet another business term that's emerged in the wired world, and is of particular interest to public relations professionals.

The term *adaptive branding* is literally about that—creating a business that has a strong stance but cannot be pigeonholed. It adapts, like the chameleon, to suit the perceptions of whatever sector you are trying to communicate with.

Amazon.com chief executive Jeff Bezos didn't call his company Books.com, even though that was their first major product offering. He knew that his business model was infinitely expandable, able to flow like the mighty river that the company is named after.

Such flexibility is crucial in a world where message points are created on the fly, without the benefit of research. What works today has to be able to work tomorrow or your business could be over.

In today's market, companies always have to have an alternate strategy. In the entire year of 1999, Business Wire distributed 531 press releases with business-to-business in the headline. From January to June 2000, over 1913 releases have been sent out with B2B in the headline, signifying the tremendous leap businesses have made to embracing the business customer.

There is no doubt those strategies will change yet again in a few months. When they do, they're going to have to make their case to the public and investors about the wisdom of their strategy.

That's where having a CEO like Bezos is a major advantage. Think about it. Here's a guy who has done nothing but lose money, and yet he's regarded as one of the leaders of the new economy, quoted or cited in almost every article that attempts to explain how the wired world is changing the brick-and-mortar world. That's adaptive.

Of course, not every business decision is made by the seat of the pants. There is a place for vision that looks beyond the next day. But how can that vision be reconciled with the need for speed?

The answer to that dilemma for public relations specialists is to remember that the world ends every 120 days. In order to accomplish any research, programs are built on dual tracks. One track is research, both traditional and nontraditional, leading to the development of key message points and positioning.

At the same time the position is being developed, there is the faster pace, writing press releases, contacting media, racing ahead of the slow and careful pace of the first track as carefully as possible. Public relations professionals today know that the full positioning of the company still isn't clear, but there's no time to wait for the concrete to harden. Companies must forge ahead. Internet time demands it.

The tracks come together after 90 days, leaving an organization right at the end of the 120-day cycle, but armed with new information that will allow management to plot and properly plan the next wave.

A good public relations program for most any company engaged in the digital world is built for the first 120 days, and then changed on a monthly basis or daily, if need be. The market evolves that rapidly.

Beyond 120 days, it is very difficult to predict where any company is going to be. If after 120 days, a brand is still clinging close to its original brand proposition business model, then this could be an early warning that something is wrong.

Of course, one of the most interesting offshoots of the digital communications game is the idea of aspirational branding. It's the kind of marketing that makes the consumer feel smart, feel cool, feel ahead of the curve just by being associated with a product or service or medium.

Consumers feel good about themselves when they're on the right side early in the game. Good branding takes that into account. It makes them feel exclusive, like they are part of a special club.

The Internet has been particularly rich soil for that sort of marketing. Just by virtue of having to access it via computer makes someone feel just a tad superior. Consumers simply click and the order is confirmed. No fighting the mobs in the malls, looking for parking, or dealing with snotty salespeople. All done from the comfort and security of your home.

A good example of an aspirational brand transitioning to the online world would be Nike. The sneaker company, known for its "swoosh" logo and its Michael Jordan ads, didn't get off on the right foot on the Internet. Although some of its initiatives were cool and cute, none were very effective. One of Nike's first ventures in the online world was designing and promoting @tlanta, a site devoted to the 1996 Summer Olympics. The site provided "editorial" commentary and updates on the Olympic events comingled with Nike product descriptions and promotional ads.

A nice idea. But the payoff for going to the URLs wasn't all that wonderful, and smacked mostly of promoting Nike. Users would visit once, but they certainly wouldn't return again and again, the ultimate goal of every web campaign.

Nike had a better idea with its "build your own sneaker" campaign. During this operation, Nike ID users who visited the Nike site could custom design a sneaker, choosing a red swoosh to go with purple laces. It was a nice, interactive touch, and proved extremely popular. But Nike appears to finally be moving its lifestyle brand into the digital space in a big way in the next few years. The company has discussed publicly plans to market connectivity devices such as digital music players. Finally, it appears the Nike brand, which stands for an active lifestyle, will attempt to become far more than a sneaker company, and will help position the company as a forward-thinking, hip part of the digital revolution. The target audience, the active lifestyle consumer, will be able to embrace the Nike brand in ways beyond stopping in the sneaker store.

Another brand making a transition with its audience in a positive way is the publication *Smart Business*. This is a ZDNet publication that was formerly known as a somewhat geeky book titled *PC Computing*, but is transforming itself into a smart, hip, forward-thinking magazine for Internet-oriented businesspeople. *Smart Business for the New Economy* answers the needs of business professionals and empowers them with strategies and solutions on using technology to help solve everyday business problems. What the company has done is focus on highly topical issues. Instead of a product-oriented brand, it's now focused on what will happen next in such hot-button issues as privacy, security, digital rights management, and other Internet staples. *Smart Business* fills the gap between computer publications, business publications, and Internet industry publications. It's the only publication that's pragmatic in nature, helping businesses make intelligent technology decisions that can assist them long term. It's now perceived as current, often ahead of the pack. Which is, of course, where businesspeople aspire to be, and *Smart Business* is positioning itself as a must read for that audience. With the shift in editorial content to a more hands-on, practical, how-to get ahead content focus, the name change to *Smart Business for the New Economy* is another step in the right direction.

Of course, the ability to be speedy and entrepreneurial and adaptive means nothing if it's done without credibility.

Credibility is something that a company either has or doesn't have. Credibility is a combination of the sustainability of a business (including its business plan, business model, and management team) coupled with market demand. Credibility adds value, and generates an audience's willingness to believe and conviction that the business will succeed.

Early in the Internet age, dot coms faced an enormous amount of skepticism on virtually every front. But particularly vexing was the idea that these sites could handle transactions with the same amount of security, privacy, and—yes—credibility as their real-world counterparts.

eBay has demonstrated that credibility is difficult but far from impossible to establish for a brand-new Internet company. It was among the first to figure out how to hold online auctions.

The whole practice hinged on one crucial aspect of the transaction: Consumers had to believe that when they bought something, they would get what they're supposed to get from the buyer. eBay devised a system where others could warn their colleagues about the reputation of the traders. It was a system that grew organically from the tools of communication, the Internet's greatest strength.

As a result of those ratings, eBay became credible, and it was legitimized as an electronic marketplace that never existed before. It has managed to not just survive but prosper in a very difficult environment.

The goal is to begin to build credibility with public relations before even putting out a press release. Public relations professionals must establish personal relationships with journalists, most desirably face to face. The client and the journalist should at least establish a level of rapport so that the journalist feels comfortable calling the client to follow up, and thinks of this person as a reasonably honest and respectable person.

To that end, it is critical for the public relations advisors to sit down with the clients and discuss credibility and how it applies to their company. Table 2-2 outlines some of the questions you should ask before representing a new initiatives.

Many start-ups looking to gain acceptance and buy-in typically feel that their strategic alliances are the greatest, hottest news story in the history of the world and they want to promote the heck out of them.

Table 2-2 The Credibility Checklist: Seven Ways to Ensure Your Company Is a Credibility Winner, Not a Credibility Loser

YES	NO	
☐	☐	Your organization's CEO/main spokesperson evokes confidence and exudes honesty and concern with all audiences.
☐	☐	All "skeletons" from the organization's past and previous management experiences have been shared with the communications team, and a contingency plan has been created to handle any volatile issues.
☐	☐	Proper customer care channels have been established online and offline.
☐	☐	The organization has, in the past, overdelivered or at least met promises.
☐	☐	The organization has the financial and industry support of third-party analysts and endorsers.
☐	☐	Employees and customers believe in the organization's goals and vision and some are willing to speak publicly.
☐	☐	You believe in the organization and what the company and its management are setting out to accomplish.

Often, the story they have in mind isn't worth the ink that it's going to be printed on, and a public relations specialist cannot, in good faith, push it to a journalist as a great story. By selling the media a false bill of goods, it will damage not just the client's reputation but also the reputation of the agency.

For agencies, the ultimate client is the journalist. If an agency loses its credibility with a journalist—it's over.

Ideally, the journalist should identify quality and honesty from the story the agency sends out. Most journalists agree that there's a tremendous amount of pressure now for agencies to put out large numbers of press releases.

That runs right into the wall created by the clients. There is a belief in the Internet community that more is better, that the more press releases a company does, the more credibility and attention it will attract.

However, journalists are tired of the uncreative, lingo-laden, impersonal drivel they receive more often than not and are beginning to get louder in their cries for help to the public relations community.

Public relations practitioners must also consider other audiences besides media when issuing a press release designed to build credibility. Next to the media, investors are probably the most important target audience. Individual and institutional investors use these releases to form their opinion of a company's performance. Until the last 2 or 3 years, when press releases were issued, they usually had a legitimate news angle, with the ultimate objective of having that story printed.

Now there are times when press releases are released solely to become archived in news release databases maintained by such services as PR Newswire or BusinessWire and serviced to online news sites like Yahoo!, Lycos, and other Internet portals, with no expectations of the content of the release being picked up by the media. In fact, in 1999, Business Wire distributed over 250,000 press releases. It is highly unlikely every one of these releases made it directly into a news story.

The reason is the investment and other business communities. When potential investors now review a stock, they will go to Yahoo! Finance and Lycos and will find a series of press releases that might have been on PR Newswire or BusinessWire. Both of those outlets are flourishing like they never have before because of the volume of releases coming from all kinds of companies, both online and offline.

That helps build credibility with a select audience, the investment community. They see the activity, form an opinion about the validity of the trend, and place their bets accordingly. This tactic is often used with prospective employees and business partners eager to conduct their due diligence using the online databases.

Credibility can also be obtained by building a strong media profile. This is trickier than servicing releases to BusinessWire and the like, but its results are very impressive.

Datek, one of the largest online brokerages, is a prime example of a business being validated through media coverage. The company was one of the early leaders in online stock trading. In the beginning of that industry, traditional businesses like Merrill Lynch and PaineWebber scoffed at Internet trading. They never believed that it would amount to anything, and, if it did, they felt that their market preeminence and established position would allow them to enter whenever they desired and dominate the market.

But the media saw it differently, and began reporting on this new trend early in the game. The media saw what Datek and related businesses like E-Trade and Ameritrade were all about, and reported on the growing boom in the online trading business to the point where it became a self-fulfilling prophecy.

Reading about these online trading sites in the media, the general investor and people who never before considered stock trading began to see the point: "Wow, these guys are for real." Thus, all of these properties, now well established in their own right, were all built on public relations.

If you remember those concentric circles from that rather boring marketing class in college, selling is simply achieved by reaching the innovator and the early adapter. Only then can a business reach the vast early majority audience. The best way to reach the innovator and early adapter is through public relations. Unfortunately, advertising is a mass communications medium, and not a good niche medium. The Internet is the ultimate niche communicator.

Credibility can carry a company a long way, even when its stories strain credibility. A case in point is Jeff Bezos.

In the spring 2000, Amazon.com was under fire from critics because of its patent on one-click purchasing. The company claimed it had developed the first method where customers could store their purchasing information online, thereby reducing the amount of time it took for them to order a product.

The idea was that if a company gave a customer less time to reconsider a purchase, its sell-through rate would increase.

There is a great deal of controversy surrounding Internet patents, particularly those involving business methods. Many argue that because the medium is so new, the patent officials whose job it is to determine whether an application is truly a unique product are overwhelmed, and are making bad decisions.

That controversy quickly stuck to Amazon.com. The publicly traded company soon learned that consumers were not enamored with its claims of innovation.

When Amazon.com was awarded its patent for one-click shopping, there was a considerable hue and cry from the companies whose business would be affected by it. That, in turn, led to considerable negative press about the implications of such patents, particularly focusing on Amazon's role.

That's where the Bezos credibility factor kicked in. He responded perfectly by coming out with a statement saying that he wanted either the length of patents to be reduced or the number to be reduced.

He completely turned around the perception that he had patented an idea that would harm the growth of the Internet by coming down on the side of those who were clamoring for change.

It's also important to note that he did that without conceding his advantage. It's a matter of taking a negative issue and making it into a positive.

That's not to say that Bezos pulled the wool over people's eyes. It's just that his believability, his sincerity, carried the day.

Credibility doesn't mean different things to different people. It's pretty cut and dried. Credibility is believability. One great example of credibility is Joe Torre, the manager of the New York Yankees. Always a stand-up guy, addressing the issues clearly and with minimal equivocation, Torre's earned a reputation for honesty. That's a change from when Billy Martin and George Steinbrenner traded anonymous verbal jabs daily in the press. Because they were so thinly veiled, it hurt their credibility.

Microsoft chairman Bill Gates has been the victim of a credibility problem, but appears to be making an effort to correct that. A now very visible Gates is appearing in television commercials, publicizing his charitable contributions, and putting a human face on what had become an increasingly monolithic company. Some people may argue that both Steve Case and Gates are merely being biased toward their companies in their public communications, slanting their utterances to more favorably reflect their positions.

It is not the right way to communicate.

Obviously, to be untruthful is suicide in terms of communications on the Internet. But being biased is not much better. It's certainly not the way to build a long-term franchise, and at some point it will come back to haunt you. Because, in the end, the truth wins out, especially on the Internet.

Individuals or companies who are perpetually biased in their statements build up a perception that gradually erodes credibility, to the point where even their most benign statements are greeted with suspicion. That's a tough position to be in when dealing with public and media perceptions, which are typically very hard to quickly turn around once they're entrenched.

At a time when the need to build credibility has become the crucial communications ingredient for success on the Internet, public relations has never mattered more. One good full-page story is worth 10 full-page ads no matter their quality. Great media can create awareness for a company instantaneously. It can legitimize the company, its management team, and its web site's products and services immediately, creating a level of public trust that allows the customer to make that leap of faith from browser to buyer.

Some things never change. Even today, the Holy Grail of building credibility through a media campaign for a new company is an article in any of the big five: *Business Week, Fortune, Forbes, The Wall Street Journal,* or *The New York Times.*

Appearing on their pages automatically and instantaneously bestows not just awareness but also credibility. While those are all brands from the traditional media, their news cycles have also been affected by the Internet's need for speed.

The New York Times and *The Wall Street Journal* are daily, but both have active and well-traveled web sites. *Business Week* is a weekly publication, but it, too, has a web site that releases articles 3 days prior to the print publication for subscribers. *Fortune* and *Forbes*, which were previously monthlies with 3- and 4-month lead times, are now bi-weeklies. Both have web sites that contribute heavily to the company's news operations.

At the same time, public relations professionals today should not rely completely on the traditional media outlets to build a credible campaign. Organizations can now almost guarantee to their boss an audience before important digital media because of their tremendous need for content, mainly because there is no set limit to the amount of pages they can produce. In addition, an emerging brand can begin to build awareness in the digital media and build a spiral campaign to print and broadcast.

In a print magazine, there is normally a 60-/40-page count ratio, editorial to advertising. Not so with *People Online* or *Business Week Online*. Without space limits, these web sites are much more open to receiving inquiries on a particular product or service.

Think about the expanded opportunities over the last few years, and it is easy to realize why publicity has become so important. The Middleberg/Ross study found that approximately 80 percent of the 300 largest newspapers in the United States now have web sites.

Of that, almost 30 percent report that more than half of their content is original. These web sites are no longer just taking stories that appear in their print publication and repurposing them for online consumption. In fact, they are adding original content in addition to some of the print stories that appear online.

So the ability to place stories online is much greater than print or broadcast. And that means far greater opportunity for public relations professionals and their clients to gain awareness and recognition in the wired world first, traditional media second.

ADVERTISING VERSUS PUBLIC RELATIONS: THE UNENDING DEBATE

Despite the fact that advertising and public relations are about finding an audience and shaping it, both are totally separate skills. Public relations people talk to journalists. Advertisers talk to customers. Public relations people talk to journalists—a highly educated audience that takes great delight in its healthy sense of skepticism. Advertising? It appeals to a different side of the brain. It seduces, trying to subliminally influence. It's a different message, a different approach. Public relations people are trying to reach a high-skill audience by breaking through the clutter in a very targeted way. Advertising, on the other hand, can often break through just by the sheer volume of buying power.

It would be wrong to say there are no collegial feelings, but these worlds are very separate in a lot of ways. Even though advertising agencies are buying public relations firms, advertisers now have more of an appreciation for the impact of public relations than they ever had because their clients are asking for it. If advertisers have good-quality public relations in their arsenal, they are considered top-shelf firms.

It used to be if a company had a new product, it would announce a $10-million advertising budget. And, oh yes, a $20,000 public relations budget for press releases.

But that has changed to the point where, now, public relations counsel is retained before advertising. The Internet and advertising are at variance, in that advertising is truly a mass-market communications tool. That's why it's ideal for television, which is a mass-market medium. The Internet is not a mass-market medium. The Internet is a niche medium, in fact, the ultimate niche medium. So advertising has had enormous difficulty succeeding because it's been using the old approaches to a different medium.

Advertisers have still not found success online. Banner ads do not work. They do not produce meaningful, measurable results. Ad agencies have to work very hard to spend a $1 million online to achieve a comparable advertising reach to television, making the jobs of media buyers that much tougher. It's a tough, low margin business for them.

Just think of it from a media agency standpoint. A firm can buy three or four television commercials at $250,000 a pop, and spend $1 million. Try and spend $1 million on advertising banners and you could eat up the better part of a week searching for the correct sites and placement.

Even if you did manage to get everything placed, it wouldn't work. Traditional advertisers have yet to truly understand the Internet.

Television commercials fill the screen, forcing consumers to watch. On the Internet, the ad is just a small part of the screen. Easily avoided. Even America Online hasn't fully grasped the concept, although it does the best job possible of grabbing a browser's attention by making sure the first thing he or she sees is an ad after logging on. The problem is that ads cannot dominate the screen the way they can dominate the television. Consumers have too many options. I'm not sure advertising through the Internet will ever be as successful as it's been on television.

Some strongly believe, yours truly among them, that most web advertising will eventually be performance-based. The most common yardstick of Internet advertising—Clicks per thousand impressions (CPM), which measures the cost of advertising for every 1000 "impressions," or viewings—will be left behind. The primary reason that companies will buy Internet advertising based on performance instead of impressions is that they have the data to make a more informed decision. Simply put, we can now acquire much more information in the advertising process than ever before. Companies such as

DoubleClick, Personify, CoreMetrics, Broadbase, and many others are helping ad buyers to rationalize their purchases.

The biggest catalyst for ad efficiency has been the near shutdown of the market for initial public offerings and the subsequent focus in the start-up world on profits and cost controls. This abrupt and refreshing change immediately tightens the belt of most Internet marketing departments and targets their spending on the most efficient forms of advertising they can find. Gone are the days when companies indiscriminately bought the "anchor tenancy" on their favorite portal just as a branding event.

While large impressions-based deals are being canceled, "per click" and "per sale" deals are flourishing. Some of the newer portals and search sites—such as Goto.com and iWon.com—are willing to do performance-based programs, and they are getting a larger percentage of the ad budgets as a result. More and more, companies are forming strong ad partnerships with such high-traffic portals. Additionally, there is a rise in CPC (cost per click) ad networks. Companies in this realm (such as ValueClick) are doing extremely well.

New variations of ad banners are emerging, such as "intermercials" and "superstitials," (both serving as short commercial clips), which can be personalized and shown at specific times during a consumer's web-surfing process. These commercials can be inserted in response to clicks on specific areas of a site or at key times during an online purchase.

Other seasoned dot coms are busy inventing new ways to push their brands under consumers' noses.

Microsoft Corp.'s Expedia travel service, for instance, in July announced that in addition to its marketing campaign, it would create a chain of Expedia.com Cafes in airports around the United States in conjunction with HMSHost, formerly Host Marriott Services.

Expedia, which has a national radio program, is also planning to launch a magazine, *Expedia Travels*, this fall.

The one thing that may work to sustain brand reliance on advertising, but hasn't happened yet, is infomercials on television to promote dot coms. Infomercials would probably be a big success because they can really spend time and go into a web site's attributes in depth. Eventually, advertisers will begin to understand that and use it as a tool to develop their clients.

The bottom line is this: If media companies want to have long-term, sustainable relationships with their customers, they need to establish win-win contracts. Otherwise, they will be stuck in the "churn and burn" mode in which they'll be constantly in search of new ad dollars.

The wireless world is another story entirely. It is where more creative things can be done because the message center is physically different. Granted, the screen is smaller, but it is more controllable.

If you think of the screen on a telephone to find out what the weather is, a browser can easily connect to a travel site. This is where content comes in, and that's what has driven public relations to be more successful than advertising. The Internet is all about content. Public relations has always been more information-driven than image-driven. Ergo, public relations will still stand out over advertising in the coming wireless universe.

Public relations, as a general rule, is a much easier process to measure results than advertising as numerous services exist to measure the relationship between the media and trends in online traffic. Online advertising, primarily through banner advertising, has long been tagged as an unproven communications tool.

In addition to the privacy issues that concern consumers, there is such an abundance of ads vying for consumer attention that it's possible users don't even notice them anymore. Even if consumers do click on banner ads, there is such a significant gap between a consumer's exposure to an online ad and the point of purchase as a result of viewing the ad, making it extremely difficult to measure ROI. As broadband providers tout "TV-like quality programming," advertisers are hoping to leverage the Internet as an advertising-ready medium, and recreate the open communications environment that TV provides.

This strategy creates a problem, however, as advertisers seek sites that provide them with targeted audiences, sometimes at the expense of online users, who could potentially be bombarded with ads. Privacy and security are also issues of concern, since advertisers do want demographics, but consumers are sometimes wary of registration and tracking processes that sites use to gather viewership information.

The growing emergence of rich media and the broadband technology supporting it is pushing advertising to a new level of interaction. Public relations is perceived to be a much easier communications tool to fully utilize the Internet's capabilities and measure how directly campaigns affect a web site. These processes have become even more productive with the help of such online distribution tools as MediaLink and such tracking services as NetCurrents. MediaLink offers clients electronic versions of such traditional public relations services as VNRs, WebCasting, and CyberMedia Tours, while NetCurrents measures traffic trends to determine the correlation between public relations efforts and the impact that they have on a site's success.

Collaborative filtering technology from NetPerceptions enables a vendor to target users with content in real time through a combination of past purchase histories, analysis of click-throughs, and answers to questionnaires. E-commerce sites can then calculate what a consumer is likely to buy, and leverage this information for recommendation and cross-selling purposes. Advertising.com uses the tracking system AdLean, which serves ads based on such data as an ad's success in attracting click-throughs. The company claims that its ads garner a click-through rate three times higher than the industry norm. In the future, there will be one other way that advertising may stand out.

To get back to our main thrust: how do you know public relations is more effective than advertising to build and transform a sustainable brand? Public relations has the ability, unlike advertising, to measure instant success. When a print or broadcast piece appears, the 800 numbers start ringing, spikes to the site start jumping up, e-commerce happens. Stock prices jump. Applications to join a company suddenly leap skyward. It's akin to the University of Wisconsin reporting that applications tripled after its football team won the Rose Bowl. It's not unusual to see a similar effect for a client based on positive stories. Their recruitment efforts also jump.

Another notably less scientific way public relations is instantly measurable is when the business begins getting calls from colleagues, acquaintances, and family members. The CEO may not remember an advertising campaign, but they will always remember the story that their roommate from business school saw about them in the local newspaper. This is affectionately known as the "you'll know" technique. Admittedly, there are numerous scientific approaches to determine whether a public relations campaign is working. However, with public relations, the "you'll know" technique is still a metric not to be ignored because the buzz factor can be overwhelming.

Of course, many dot-com companies don't have the kind of money needed to make an impact through advertising. So public relations becomes the default medium of choice because it is relatively less expensive in cost. There are times where, admittedly, advertising has done a good job, a job that public relations probably couldn't do. But that tends to be for more mature companies and more mature industries.

Computer-chip manufacturer Intel, with its famous "Intel Inside" program, is one of the best examples. (See Figure 3-1.) Intel was in danger of seeing its chip business become commoditized. It was blending together with far too many other chips, to the point where it didn't matter to the consumers what they had in their machines. Intel's ad campaign changed that. Their advertising was directed to make the chip a demanded product. It went from being something no one cared about to the point where people demanded to have the Intel chip specifically.

That's a textbook example of advertising winning over public relations. When companies become larger and they need to reach a large mass audience with a simple, single message, advertising is very effective. When companies are first building their Internet businesses or transforming into e-businesseses, it does not make much sense to advertise in a mass-market way. They're going to reach too many uninterested parties.

Figure 3-1

*   *   *

Public relations, of course, is the most economical route to generate attention. But this is not to say that one shouldn't do advertising. Early on, it's just economically stupid. It just doesn't make sense to spend too much of a company's formation capital in the advertising world when there's public relations, direct mail, viral marketing, and many other more cost-effective approaches. But at some point, a blend becomes practical.

A good illustration of how targeted, integrated public relations programs can be more effective than ad campaigns can be illustrated by using a fictitious company, StartupRewards.com, a technology services provider in the sales and marketing incentive business.

StartupReward's services are designed to encourage salespeople to reach or exceed sales targets, and if they do, they will be rewarded. It is also a company that allows customers, such as frequent buyers, to, in effect, purchase credits much like they would purchase frequent-flier miles or online currency. Often they can get loyalty rewards through this web site, making it both a B2B and a B2C site.

This is not an actual company, but an amalgam of several real-life businesses. We'll show how the company missed several opportunities to get public relations.

Let's assume the company said that it was not happy with its awareness levels. Not only that, it felt that people did not understand it. As a result, they planned to spend several million dollars in advertising to get their message out to the public.

What our fictional company missed, though, are several ways to pocket that million dollars and get free advertising—i.e., publicity—by just recognizing how good several of their own stories are.

First, there is an opportunity for media attention stemming from the fact that this company is moving from a consumer play to a B2B play. For a time, it was a defining trend in the Internet industry. A savvy public relations professional could have taken that ball and run with it.

Another possible story that could have resulted in a story was the company's technology.

Given that it had a lot of blue chip customers on the corporate side, and key corporate investors, part of their story is the great technology it uses, far exceeding anybody else's in the space, and its platform that empowers merchants to make changes to its promotions and rewards. The merchant can make changes right on the site, and extend their consumer programs to brick and mortar stores.

Finally, the company has a great financial model. Consumers and businesses are given incentives to use its services. Therefore, downturns in either sector will have less of an impact on the overall revenue, and, in fact, its incentives are the type that will attract more customers in down times. All of this makes for a great stories. And it won't cost millions of dollars to generate a return.

Picking out great stories isn't always easy. In fact, even with the multitude of angles on StartupRewards.com, the press might balk. The reason? As varied as the story angles pitched. The media might note that the company hasn't made money, and, because of that, the stock has been hit hard. They might also mention that the online incentives market is very crowded. They may also have hardened perceptions of previously failed reward programs.

These problems can be overcome. But it takes a unique skill to focus journalists away from the negative and get them to pay attention to the heart of a story, especially in a field that can often be confusing, such as incentive marketing.

First, let's deal with the perception problem. A savvy public relations professional would know that even though Startup Rewards.com's competitors were pale imitators, it is critical to do more than tell journalists that. You need evidence, and that comes from third-party stakeholders. The public relations professional seeking to combat the problem might first properly position the company with financial analysts and industry analysts. They, in turn, will help influence the journalists, who usually need to be dragged, kicking and screaming, away from assumptions, which are set in cement quite early in a company's life.

Besides getting third-party influencers on your side, one other way to change those assumptions is, in effect, to ignore them. Rather, the company needs to reposition itself for the next stage, one that would marry the online world and the offline world. That takes the story from a recap to a tale of a company's progress in coping with a changing marketplace, always a good story on the Internet beat.

Getting the financial press going on StartupRewards.com requires yet another tactic. One way would be to point out a company's market penetration over its stock price. Financial analysts usually love market penetration, and it will be a good way to bring them aboard. That will make it easier to turn the financial press on to more key third-party spokespersons.

The end result? Once these messages were received and positive stories were generated, investors would likely come back. Thus, proving once again the power of public relations.

A savvy public relations advisor would undoubtedly recommend the company take a leadership role in its sector by creating some original research. It is a great tool to establish leadership. In the case of our fictional company, StartupRewards.com, the topic could be something of critical importance to emerging and traditional businesses alike, akin to "How do you use the Internet to increase sales performance?"

That research provides fodder for future speaking appearances and large amounts of future publicity because journalists respond well to a credible research study that helps them understand the context of the business's offerings and trends in business activity in the Internet era. In addition, a well-conducted research study provides irrefutable data by an independent body that helps shape a story and give it newsworthy significance. All of this would be designed to position this company as a leader in its field.

In summary, public relations is the tool to use if you want to reach a specific audience at a reasonable cost. Advertising is the tool to use when you need to reach a mass audience and have a budget that can tolerate the high levels of investment. But there is one other major differentiator between public relations and advertising. One of the keys to establishing any company is the implanting of its brand into the consumer and business conscience. Our colleagues in advertising are focused on a brand's essence. With public relations, brand can mean something quite different. Public relations branding is aspirational. It focuses on painting a brand into a truly contextual story, creating a real picture of how a business fits into the greater marketplace. Now, let's take a look at the way public relations has changed branding tactics in the wired world.

WHO YOU ARE TODAY MAY HAVE NO EFFECT ON WHO YOU ARE TOMORROW: BRANDING IN THE NEW ECONOMY

Determining how to create and build a brand that will stand out in the Internet marketplace is not for the faint of heart. Sustainable brands are not developed overnight but instead require consistent tending and development as well as the support and foundation to evolve into a killer brand that can lead not just today but also tomorrow. Let's take a quick look at how two companies—one old, one new—"got it" and how their strategies represent a larger wave that calls for critical business reliance on brand development.

Cisco, which is, today, the world's largest commerce site, is a traditional turned Internet brand that has earned numerous industry awards and accolades for its pioneering Internet business focus and web-based customer service. Since shipping its first product in 1986, the company has grown into a global market leader that holds No. 1 or No. 2 market share in virtually every market segment in which it participates. At the basis of Cisco's success has been its decision to adopt the brand-owning model and shed its traditional role as an equipment manufacturer. Today outside suppliers directly fill 55 percent of Cisco's orders. Thus, Cisco is able to leverage both its physical and human capital by integrating outside companies into its supply chain. Companies like Cisco and Dell are "brand-owning companies." They are selling customer satisfaction.

The transformation is even more startling when one looks at the widespread effect this evolution is having on business as a whole and at what some of the more progressive, yet traditional, companies like Ford are doing.

In the past few years, Ford, the largest truck maker and second largest auto manufacturer, has spent well over $12 billion to acquire prestigious brand names: Jaguar, Aston Martin, Volvo, and Land Rover. None of these marquees brought much in the way of plant and equipment, but plant and equipment isn't what the new business model is about. It's about brands and brand building and consumer relationships.

By 2010, companies like Ford will look more like companies like Cisco. Instead of manufacturing, Ford will outsource over the Internet. Using the Internet, Ford and other companies hope to change from a push model to a pull model. Instead of a manufacturer pushing product out to the consumer, the consumer—stimulated, of course, by smart public relations and marketing—will pull product through the supply chain. This dramatic business turn is symbolic of not only the current trends but also the future change that investment companies in transition will need to make in their brand in order to succeed according to new rules of doing business.

Every successful brand in the Internet economy can be evaluated using four metrics:

- *Leadership*: Brand leadership means that your key audiences believe you are the No. 1 brand in your space. Developing that perception is crucial. If a consumer is going to buy a computer, which computer do they buy? Will it be Dell, Compaq, or some computer company that's no longer around? Naturally, the choice of most is the firm considered a leader.

- *Financial relevance*: Financial relevance is determined by perceptions of whether a firm is going to be here a year from now. Again, most consumers and businesses want to deal with a firm that appears, at the least, to be well managed, well financed, financially secure, and has a decent business plan, or has access to cash that will allow it to continue indefinitely. Amazon and iVillage and probably half the Internet companies out there are not making any money. So they better have solid sources of capital and the perception that they will be around for the long haul.

- *Cachet*: Cachet is a fleeting, ephemeral type of feeling that public relations helps build. Cachet is cool, it's of the moment, and it's just as easily lost. Cadillac used to have cachet; it doesn't anymore. Certain health foods used to have cachet and now they don't. The wearing of a fur coat used to have cachet, then it didn't, but now it's beginning to again.

- *Status*: Status is more permanent than cachet. It's what you have as a clear market leader. Dell has status. Apple has status. MTV has status.

If a company can create a space for itself in the first three metrics, it has a fairly good chance of reaching status. But there are many pitfalls and perils on the road to that lofty perch. Let's examine a few of them.

In today's technology-focused economy, the consumer and business executive are confronted with an onslaught of companies and brands. Each purports to offer "cutting-edge" products that attempt to transform one's life and provide unimaginable convenience and satisfaction.

Of course, a lot of the claims fall far short of delivering on the promise. But one company that has taken the ideas of fast, sleek, and cool to the next level is Sony and their line of Vaio computer products.

Sony Vaio, shown in Figure 4-1, which entered the PC computing market as a line of state-of-the-art, multimedia notebook computers in 1996, has now expanded to MP3 players, and its Internet site is starting to resemble the functions of a lifestyle portal, where consumers can immerse themselves

Figure 4-1

in the most current technology, news, and offerings from Sony Vaio.

What Sony has done is use the Vaio product line as a branding and imaging tool to leverage some of their top selling and most innovative products, taking the name beyond computers into a different realm. This aspirational brand positioning now focuses on the "tech savvy" consumer and business professional who feels a need to be in touch with the latest trends in technology, electronics, and computers.

Yes, Sony Vaio is a high-end product with high-end costs attached. But in expanding upon the highly respected and reputable Sony brand name, the electronics giant has created a lifestyle portal centered upon the "next-generation" Sony Vaio image, one that a certain segment of free-spending consumers purportedly cannot live without. It makes them feel exclusive, part of a special club.

The Internet has been particularly rich soil for that sort of marketing. The very nature of the medium is part of that. Consumers, by virtue of having to access the Internet via computer, automatically feel just a tad superior.

Sony's Vaio campaign underlines a significant point: good public relations strategy must be flexible. The really smart companies constantly reinvent and/or reposition themselves in the media, and need public relations counsel that can move with them, reacting to the constantly changing climate by properly positioning the companies in line with the trends of the moment.

A classic example is Oracle, which has gone from a software company to an Internet e-commerce company in the last few years. Oracle chairman Larry Ellison, as of this writing, is now richer than Microsoft chairman Bill Gates. It's because his company has been able to thrive in a changing environment.

The sort of manipulation that comes with constantly shifting perception at times seems obvious, but there is no choice, and companies that do it have plenty of peers moving with them. All of them have to change, because: (1) it's good marketing and (2) it's good financial communications.

In today's ever-shifting economy, it's important to go with what's hot at the moment. For a lot of companies, that's meant repositioning themselves as Internet companies.

Such "rebranding" of a company sometimes has little to do with a specific product or business. Sometimes, it's done for the sake of investors or, in the case of Microsoft, to change public perception.

The media have shown great capacity to let companies reinvent themselves. Companies such as IBM, once a stodgy dinosaur that seemed tied to mainframe computers in a desktop computer age, have been written off in the past only to use public relations and advertising to rise again.

Anyone not convinced that brand matters on the Internet should look at the June 2000 Jupiter Communications report that states that consumers prefer familiar traditional brands to new pure-play brands by a ratio of 4 to 1. A number of exceptions exist—most of them have succeeded in large part through effective public relations.

The repositioning of companies in the marketplace became particularly acute at the height of the Internet frenzy. By the late 1990s, companies that were tying their futures to the Internet were still getting high market valuations, even as good, solid traditional businesses and even some software companies lagged. Realizing that "irrational exuberance" over the Internet was driving the market, some companies felt it was simply a question of going to the high ground, and the high ground at that point in time was to position oneself as an Internet company. Many did so, and some were quite successful.

That is not to say that a company can magically declare itself an Internet company, reap the public relations benefits, and automatically experience a stock surge. The public isn't fooled quite that easily.

In fact, some companies have tried that tactic and failed miserably.

The classic example of such hubris is a company out of Dallas called Zapata, which was best known as a manufacturer of fish food. Suddenly, out of the blue and at the height of the stock market's Internet frenzy, Zapata's chairman declared that the company was going to become an Internet company by buying up established Internet sites and combining them into a portal.

For weeks after that announcement, the news media buzzed with talk about Zapata. Who were they? Why were they doing this? And most importantly, could they pull it off?

The market absolutely didn't buy it. They did not budge on the stock valuation for Zapata that was needed to make the necessary acquisitions via stock swaps. Eventually, shortly after creating a frenzy merely by announcing its plans and acquiring a few sites, Zapata backed off from its declarations and went back to being a regular, boring old company. That proves once again that just because you declare you will build it, it doesn't mean the investors will come.

An example of a company doing it the right way is CMGI, which started quietly but built a network of family companies that were consistent with the framework of the original unit. The change was gradual, evolutionary rather than revolutionary, and the public ran with the company as it grew to its current high-valuation and prominent stature within the Internet industry.

Another interesting example of an evolution in public perception—and, hence, a repositioning of the brand—is the Microsoft approach. Their communications strategy has totally changed from what it was because of the federal antitrust trial.

In late 1999, Microsoft was truly all of the things that they were presented by their enemies to be: they were arrogant, they were very aggressive, and they were way out there in their attempts to undermine competitors.

Of course, there was a good side to such zeal: their introduction of Windows 98 was one of the great new product introductions probably of the last 50 years. An unbelievable success story. They had events planned around the world, actually based on a single day.

When dawn broke in New Zealand, the first copy of Windows 98 was sold. All around the world, there were banners, balloons, Bill Gates making personal appearances, and scores of public relations firms hired to promote the event, to say nothing of the kind of dollars spent on advertising and just general promotion.

They also did a beautiful job of creating a high level of anticipation through press releases and advance news stories. They leaked information about new product features so that they gradually built up a sense of "wow," which is what this game is all about. The sense of buzz was enormous.

But then the government got involved, and a side of Microsoft that wasn't so friendly and fuzzy began to dominate the news. The legendary Microsoft zeal was channeled in a new direction to combat this threat.

They created an almost octopuslike strategy, roughly eight different strategies, all of them aimed at the same objective: soften the public perception of Microsoft.

One of their areas of focus was charitable giving. They turned attention toward the Bill Gates Foundation, run not by some corporate geek, but his wife and his wife's parents. Pretty smart move. A move that brought to light the family-oriented side of this previously monolithic corporation.

Microsoft also began to get heavily involved in Washington lobbying. It came to the point where Bill Gates' lieutenants approached George W. Bush's chief lobbyists, all aimed at hopefully influencing Bush. But, at the same time such overtures were made, Microsoft was giving heavily to both Democrats and Republicans. And Gates was making frequent forays to Washington, D.C.

Another focus was the Microsoft web site. It became the most comprehensive web site on the Microsoft monopoly trial available to anyone, anywhere. To their credit, they took the position that, good news or bad, they would make all the information available on the Microsoft site.

Why? Because their strategy is that they want people to come to their web site before they go to anybody else's. To accomplish that, Microsoft knew that they would have to have complete information, not merely a rehash of company positions. So they're making their web site the first place to go for news and information, and it's working. A tone of casual corporate openness and honesty is communicated throughout every aspect of the Microsoft legal site.

Another prong of Microsoft's plan was orchestrating responses immediately after the government's announcements. It became so commonplace that it resembled the president giving a State of the Union address, immediately followed by the opposition stating its case.

Finally, the Microsoft strategy even got to the point where Gates got a haircut and a new suit, really spiffing up his act from the total nerd he once appeared as to something resembling a half-way geek.

One other non-public relations move Microsoft used were commercials that spoke of all the wonderful things that Microsoft has done and how it has enhanced competition.

Taken together, Microsoft managed to find many new ways to get its message across. It remains to be seen how effective that is in rebranding the company for the long term, but they are really becoming a full-scale communications machine. And that's bound to help them no matter what the future holds for the company.

Not coincidentally, the Internet emerged at a time of great financial prosperity. As consumers began to spend more in the medium, marketers unleashed a massive attack of advertising. The brand wars were on.

Today, cyberspace ads are everywhere—attached to e-mails, printed on the back of concert tickets, and stuffed into electricity bills. Anyone driving into San Francisco through Silicon Valley on Highway 101 is forced to notice new billboards popping up like daisies on the side of the road. More than ever, ads interrupt a commuter's favorite morning drive-time radio show, and magazines are positively fat with ads. TV shows are actually shorter because of the number of Fidelity, Lexus, and Geico insurance ads vying for consumer attention.

Every company is striving to build its brand, and gain that elusive emotional connection between a name and a consumer.

Dot coms of all shapes and sizes joined the fray to compete for the brand loyalties of the public.

As the competition grew, so did the amount of advertising inundating the consumer. Way back when, in 1998, there were no dot-com ads in the Super Bowl. However, 1999's game boasted three dot-com ads, which grew to 17 in 2000.

However, few viewers remembered the actual brand names (not to mention what they were supposed to buy), and even fewer felt a closer connection to the companies. What they did remember were the dot-com suffixes. It wasn't until they read the local paper the next day that they began to connect the images to the brands and remember the names.

While the Super Bowl slots represented only one advertisement (in a space where frequency counts), the lack of consumer awareness was yet another affirmation of the strength of publicity, and confirmed that public relations now had a strong role in branding, long the domain of advertising.

The Super Bowl phenomena underscores that consumers are now tuning out ads as if they had selective radar. If ads for a particular sector are ubiquitous—whether it's ice cream or the Internet—they inevitably lose their power. The overall lack of response to Internet banner advertising is living proof of that.

In fact, the advertisements at Super Bowl XXXIV were, in many ways, secondary to the publicity surrounding the ads. Companies spent weeks touting the ads that would appear during the Super Bowl, often teasing consumers and the trade press with hints about what they could see. But in the end, most commercials blurred together, as there was too much information for most consumers to process in a short time span.

As a result, consumers needed news stories to remind them of what they had seen, and undoubtedly played a strong role in the ultimate decision of what to buy and what not to buy.

Let's examine the strategy of a Super Bowl advertisement from one company's perspective.

OnMoney.com, an online personal finance site, kicked off a $30-million broadcast, print, and radio advertising campaign with a commercial during Super Bowl XXXIV that coincided with the launch of the site.

The company said it chose to go with a Super Bowl ad because it not only gave them access to a wide audience, but also allowed it to use the publicity surrounding Super Bowl advertising to get further news about its launch out.

To further its efforts, OnMoney.com developed a short feature, "The Making of the Commercial," while the actual ad was being produced. Through extensive media outreach and use of the video as a pitching tool, the company's public relations agency was able to secure tremendous press coverage, including *The Wall Street Journal, USA Today, The Financial Times, The New York Times,* and over 30 broadcast TV placements in regional markets. Thus, OnMoney.com produced a clever ad campaign in order to garner media attention and begin a solid relationship with key Internet and business journalists who would be key in the company's growth and future success.

While the sheer number of new companies vying for attention has made it tougher than ever to cut through the clutter, the rise of the Internet has also allowed brands to be built faster than ever before.

Public relations is a key to that. Because there were so many more news outlets, coverage shows up a lot sooner than in the old days of monthly news cycles and three broadcast outlets. And because customers can be more easily targeted via e-mail on a one-to-one basis, or through messages boards on a slightly less direct but no less focused approach, an audience for a new brand can be created far more quickly than ever before.

That said, there are no real shortcuts to branding, even given the focus of the Internet. Brand building is still about repetition, building consensus, gaining good news reports and word of mouth, and devising ways to become a market leader.

However, smart public relations professionals and their clients are taking a new approach to branding based on an understanding of the power of public relations in building brands quickly.

First, in approaching a company's branding and positioning, it is important to immediately separate the "public relations" brand from the "advertising" brand, a concept alluded to in the previous chapter. What that means is that the two areas attack different audiences, and will build a different impression for their constituencies, thus, in effect, creating two brands.

While it is vital that the two are consistent, the public relations brand should not be beholden to the advertising brand. It must chart its own course, perhaps highlighting different features of the product, its executive team, or its place in the market. These tactics may leave the advertising team a little uneasy. That's to be expected, and should not affect the public relations team's plans.

While advertising brands are representational, emotional, and visual, public relations brands have to be sold to journalists and analysts who don't have the time or interest to listen to a company's marketing hype. Instead, successful brands must be literal, contextual, and informational. These differences are shown in Table 4-1.

In public relations branding, the traditional approach of research and testing followed by branding maintenance does not work. By the time you research a brand, the landscape has most likely changed, and the company could lose its branding opportunity to its competitors. Thus, public relations must forge ahead at a faster pace than advertising.

My agency, Middleberg Euro devised an approach to building public relations brands in the Internet economy—an adaptation (naturally) of adaptive branding. It is based on the following tenets.

Table 4-1 Advertising vs. Public Relations – The Unending Dynamic Debate

Advertising	Public relations
Brand emotion	Brand logic
Subliminal influence	Literal
Volume/frequency	Contextual
Representational	Informational
Visual	Must convey a story
Unproven targeting efficiency and effectiveness	More targeted

THREE IS THE MAGIC NUMBER

In public relations, a brand can be more complex than an advertising brand. Instead of one emotion, public relations brands try to stand for three key messages, focusing on whatever points the company feels underline its business objectives. These messages should represent the highest common denominator of understanding for all of the key media constituencies—print, broadcast, and Internet. In great interviews, time after time, the company's spokesperson should carry forth these messages as if his or her life and company depend on them.

BRAND METRICS

Every brand in the new economy is fighting to establish credibility. As such, they all need to be buttressed by numbers that validate the brand. Those numbers can include traffic, sales, share value, or years in business. Given the amount of information that journalists receive, they need those numbers in order to make the decision to write about company A instead of company B. For example, even large brands, such as Sony and IBM, must earn their stripes as Internet companies before customers will think of them in that context. Smaller Internet companies, such as Kozmo.com and eToys, have to convince customers that they are reliable enough to trust with a consumer's information. As such, every brand must have one or more metric that validates its leadership.

CATEGORY LEADERSHIP

One of the reasons branding in public relations is more difficult isn't only because of speed and clutter. It's also because business is more complex. When the financial market convulsed in April 2000, battering hi-tech stocks in particular, the conventional wisdom said that only the category leaders would survive on the Internet. Although the shakeout is not complete, it appears that this wisdom is holding true.

Brands are also constantly reinventing themselves, shape shifting on the playing field and making it extremely difficult for companies that aren't fast to adapt. For example, Nike is now offering Internet connectivity. Amazon.com does not just sell books. The *Encyclopaedia Britannica* is now free.

As a result, leadership of a category becomes more important because consumers and other businesses need to put companies into buckets in order to understand them. While not every company can be a leader in the large-category buckets, many of them can become category leaders in smaller subsets. By becoming leaders in that smaller subset, they can then leverage that brand equity and awareness into an increasingly larger or new category. In this way, smart entrepreneurial companies are using public relations to define their category, serve as the market educator, and, as a result, ensure that they are relevant.

Journalists often complain that companies talk too much about themselves. The best way to position a company one on one is to explain its relevance by first explaining the entire category landscape. In today's public relations, brands must be relevant to the larger story of the Internet economy trends for the media to pursue writing about them. As category leaders, their news strategically addresses not only how the news impacts the company but also, as the market leader, how their news impacts the entire category.

LEXICON

Internet buzzwords are death to any good positioning. Buzzwords immediately make a brand feel stale, mainly because buzzwords quickly go in and out of fashion. Journalists have developed special radar for them, and have largely learned to tune them out, thwarting a company's larger objectives in public relations.

However, in a hyperactive marketplace such as the Internet, stakeholders are looking for anything that helps define a company's leadership, innovation, or relevance.

As such, lexicon (not buzzwords) has become an important technique in branding. By creating or being the first to serve as the example of a piece of lexicon that stands for a business model, challenge, or marketplace situation is incredibly valuable.

Think of Amazon picking "e-commerce" as the defining word of its business. IBM selecting "e-business." Yahoo! defining what a "portal" would become. Or IdeaLabs terming its start-up business foundation an "incubator." Those are terms that came to define whole categories of businesses, and these companies are largely credited as the early adopters.

Public relations specialists should be reading financial and industry analyst reports and combing media articles to pick up the next wave. And as in the development of a category, coverage about companies embracing the new lexicon must then mention the company that pioneered the lexicon's new words. In this way brands are built quickly.

BUZZ

Consumers want to know what is new and cool. New and cool is often measured by "the buzz," i.e., who is talking about what. Anyone interested in building a brand should address building buzz, though frankly, it's always easier said than done.

Buzz is built in no particular standard formula. But in the Internet space, the attempts usually involve two methods.

First, it often starts with getting the information in the hands of the influencers—analysts, digerati, writers, media, and, yes, top marketing professionals.

In San Francisco, public relations professionals work the Internet party scene hard to leak information to the tastemakers. The rooftop parties on Friday nights at Internet-centric trade magazine *The Industry Standard* quickly became musts for hot companies trying to get the word out. In New York, local new media events, such as the New York New Media Association's "CyberSuds" get-together, were great places to set off early buzz on a project.

More important than the party circuit, buzz is now being cultivated online by savvy public relations professionals. Postings to newsgroups, working message boards, intentionally leaking news to online outlets and newsletters are among the preferred methods of massaging news, hoping to create a spark of interest.

To create buzz, one must monitor what's being said online. Create a list of the hot outlets in the space, from listservs to web sites, to monitor the buzz, being ready to fan a small fire to make it bigger. How many times have you heard that a company (let's call it Red Hat) is a hot company (brand) but you don't know what they actually do? Well, that's the buzz of a brand. And that's where a public relations professional can turn a spark into a fire.

CONTEXTUALIZATION

In a world moving at Internet speed, new trends, terms, competitors, issues, and lexicon are emerging on a quarterly or monthly or sometimes daily and hourly basis.

While the brand essence for companies stays the same, the actual messages we are taking to the market must change at an even faster pace. If a business's No. 1 competitor buys its No. 2 competitor, it would be naive to think that messages would not change that day, that instant, upon hearing the news.

While the advertising brand won't necessarily change, the brand communicated to the media will be altered by that news, either by public relations professionals if the company is smart and fast or by competitors if it is dumb and slow.

Smart companies understand speed and the need to quickly contextualize the transformed brand, making it relevant by ensuring that the messages match the new landscape. To be relevant, a company must think first about the larger trends and then ensure that its key messages fit into those trends. If they don't, it's time to create new messages. A brand must be deliberately connected to the larger issues beyond a single company and one narrow vertical or run the risk of being perceived as "old school" well before its time.

THE CEO AS STAR

We'll discuss this in detail in a later chapter. But the simplest way to build equity in a brand is to build equity in an individual. Think of any successful brand and you will think of a successful CEO. America Online is Steve Case. Amazon.com is Jeff Bezos. CMGI equals David Wetherell. IBM means Lou Gerstner. GE is the essence of Jack Welch.

FREQUENCY

Silence equals death in Internet times. Since everything is moving quickly, it is vital to communicate frequently. As in advertising, frequency matters.

It is especially true in public relations. Frequency allows companies to institutionalize brand perceptions in the media and provides benchmarks to know when their brand messages should change. However, smart companies also know that a press release is no longer just for media relations—it's also used to maintain general communication to stakeholders.

FINANCIAL BRANDS

Many brands are known principally for their financial performance. In this new economy, that is a risky proposition. However, stock performance is indeed a key metric.

It is recommend that investor relations (IR) and public relations (PR) be separated. This allows the public relations to carve out an identity that is not solely based on messages to Wall Street, much as advertising targets a different audience than public relations.

In this way we protect the brand from becoming too narrow and susceptible should the market perception shift.

Let's examine two different companies and their efforts in branding. Both case studies will show how fragile an image is in the marketplace.

CDNow was, at one time, the unquestioned market leader in online compact disc sales and a voice of e-commerce. Founded by twin brothers Matt and Jason Olim, the company grew from their parents' basement into a big company that specialized in delivering a vast selection of compact discs via mail order, becoming known as one of the superstores of the Internet.

But one of the biggest rules of branding is that a company has to stay active. The Internet marketplace shifts so frequently that standing still is actually akin to moving backward. A business must constantly reinvent and reposition its brand within the shifting landscape.

Unfortunately, CDNow became trapped in merger negotiation with its archrival on the Internet, N2K's Music Boulevard. At first, the marriage looked like a sheer winner—N2K had also built an impressive system of delivering CDs to the home, and also had content in the form of a well-respected news operation.

As was typical for start-ups then and now in the Internet economy, both companies were losing vast amounts of money. Thus, the decision to merge seemed smart, marrying the No. 1 and No. 2 businesses in the category.

However, the quiet period after the merger extended far too long, and both companies soon fell off the radar of journalists. While the CDNow executives were studying and researching the best ways to present the newly combined company, the marketplace shifted. Digital distribution of music became the hot-button issue, and stores that sold CDs were perceived as last year's news.

Instead of seizing the high ground and serving as the educator to journalists about the ramifications of digital distribution of music, CDNow stuck to its original vision. They insisted on defining themselves as an e-commerce business, and failed to position themselves as part of the larger digital debate that was raging.

As a result, CDNow lost its context. By the time they were finished redefining the newly merged company, they had been passed by, and other innovators had taken over as the market leaders. CDNow was recently sold to the giant German media conglomerate, Bertelsmann, at a bargain basement price of $3 per share.

*　　*　　*

The Industry Standard is a magazine that had not only perfect timing but also a fine ear for the nuances involved in creating a new brand in a crowded space.

There have been computer and Internet trade magazines for as long as both industries have existed. But like many trades, they were observers of the scene rather than part of it. Not so *The Industry Standard*.

Right from its launch, *The Industry Standard* created a differentiation for itself: it was the voice and Bible of the new economy, and served as the market educator for numerous tastemakers with its authoritative, yet wry, takes on the changes gripping the roiling seas of the scene.

But *The Industry Standard* was more than a publication. It was a new type of media company, offering professional services, e-mail newsletters, conferences, and a web site.

It became virtually one-stop shopping for all things related to this fast-paced field. In one of publishing's great success stories, *The Industry Standard* grew from its initial 24 pages to a 400-page monolith fat with advertisements, a must-read for anyone doing business on the Internet.

In short, *The Industry Standard* made all the right moves. It helped invent and disseminate the lexicon of emerging Internet categories, evangelized new developments at the hottest companies in the sector, and educated journalists and other tastemakers covering the space, helping them understand and map the changes affecting business on the Internet.

Both of these companies point out the need to change on the fly in the Internet age. But public relations professionals have another community that they must constantly monitor and adjust to—the media.

THE CURRENCY OF MEDIA

So far we've placed a lot of emphasis on the new roles for public relations professionals as counselors, strategists, intelligence gatherers, rainmakers, and web business builders. Truly, the public relations professional in the wired world is all of that—and more.

But, to be sure, the role of the public relations practitioner as media relations expert and conduit has never been more valuable. As the importance of the media continues to increase, so, too, does the role of the public relations professional change and expand.

This change is based not only on the needs of new audiences but also on the new needs of the media. For example, when today's journalists are obtaining information, often on deadline and with little research support (remember most publication and broadcast outlets work with very thin staffs), it's very difficult for them to separate accurate, timely information from that which is wrong and out of date.

Journalists are constantly looking to industry and financial analysts, the industry endorsers, the academics, the influencers, to provide context. Thus, the public relations professional must have a ready storehouse of accessible experts who can validate or reject a journalist's thesis. These must be people who can be reached, online or off—deadline demands require it. Therefore, the new climate of media relations is one that holds paramount the immediacy of information, context, and trust.

*   *   *

Let's talk a little about the differences between how the media covers technology and the Internet.

Prior to the early part of 2000, there were clear distinctions among journalists. In fact, there were clear distinctions among Internet journalists versus print journalists at the same publication.

The best example of that was *CyberTimes*, the online arm of *The New York Times*. *CyberTimes* had as many as 20 journalists reporting solely online. In a very short period, that changed.

Now, *CyberTimes* no longer exists. It's known as the *NYTimes.com*, and journalists who write for the online version are the same journalists who write for the print version. That means agencies are pitching the same person, where before they would have to pitch to two people.

As the online presence of traditional media and the scope of its coverage have expanded, the importance of the technology trade press has lessened. At one time, the trade magazine *Internet World* was a critical publication for anyone interested in getting a message across about how they moved into the digital space. But *Internet World* has largely been supplanted by more business-oriented publications, including *Business 2.0*, *The Industry Standard*, or CMP Publications' *Smart Business*. With the appearance of these new publications, there is now increased competition to cover a story about a digital company. That presents both great news—there's more outlets—and bad news—there's more confusion about the proper forum for a particular story.

Let's say a company like Sony, a company that transcends a number of industries, wants to communicate its new direction in relation to Internet gaming. Who does the agency contact about the story? Does it go to the electronics reporter? Does it go to the consumer reporter? Does it go to the Internet reporter? Does it go to the business reporter? Adding to the dilemma, very often reporters within the same publication will compete with one another for the story. So the responsibility on the public relations practitioner to know whom to give the story to within a publication has increased. If the wrong person gets the story, that public relations specialist could literally be shut out from other reporters for his career. In some ways, media relations has become a real devil's dance, and public relations professionals really need to work it carefully. Before the Internet, most publications had one journalist who covered a company. Now, it's very different, and making the wrong turn presents new dangers when liaising within a publication.

In part due to this new level of competition within the media, the use of exclusives, particularly when launching a web site, has become vital. An *exclusive* is defined as a news item prereleased to only one journalist at one publication who, in turn, produces an article with relative substance. A company can no longer just send out a general press release and expect a thousand stories. It cannot call a press conference in a convenient location with slide shows and giveaway mouse pads and expect the press to show up in droves, because a new web site is no longer newsworthy in and of itself. The game is now how an agency makes something particularly interesting and how that business works journalists vis-à-vis exclusives.

Creative public relations practitioners will target multiple exclusives with different angles, for example. One exclusive can be a technology story; one can be a business story; one can be a personality story. Each can go to a different person at a different publication. Very often, media specializing in the digital economy, like CNET or CNBC's Squawk-box, becomes more critical in many ways than getting on a more widely seen show like NBC's *Today*. That's because the audience on CNET or CNBC is so important to spreading the message. One CEO is worth a thousand raving teens when it comes to moving the market.

So how do small companies compete if they lack the marketing muscle of Microsoft but have a great story? There are ways to use Microsoft's tactics with one-hundredth the budget. (See Table 5-1.) Like Microsoft, each company has two choices—the work can be done in house or it can hire a public relations agency. Microsoft, as is true for many large companies, does both. Whatever the company's choice, it's important to have public relations people on board who have access and the skill to approach key journalists, whether they be at *Upside*, *Red Herring*, or *Fast Company*. These are exactly the kinds of publications that are read by today's business leaders, the digerati, of the Internet space. The first task in achieving great public relations on a budget is to win over the key industry trade publications. Those publications focus on the business aspects of the Internet as opposed to the technological innovation. *Red Herring, Business 2.0, The Industry Standard, Upside, Wired, Internet World, Internet Week, Smart Money*—all are read by more traditional and broadcast journalists, and provide fertile soil for larger stories in bigger publications.

It is also important to consider, perhaps even prior to contacting those publications, working with online publications. Marketing stories may be more appropriately sent to *Iconocast* or *Channel Seven*—two influential online newsletters reaching out to the Internet marketing community. From there, the next step would be to place a story with a business/financial slant in CBS *MarketWatch* or *Bloomberg Online* or *The Street.com*, the upper crust of the online financial world. This is a step-by-step process that moves quickly upon execution, but recognize that it's much easier to approach a *Business Week* or *Barron's* after being published in an Internet trade publication than going to them with no prior publicity at all.

Smooth media relations is only possible with a trained, confident company spokesperson who emits the personality of his or her business by communications message and style. For newer CEOs, it's getting a lot harder to be invited to appear on television because there are more big-name people who suddenly understand the value of being on these specialized shows, and are clamoring for positions. Not long ago, Sandy Weil, CEO of Citibank, appeared on CNN at 6:30 a.m. New York time. Unbelievable. That would never happen in the good old days. Weil believed his stock price was undervalued, so he was determined to get his company's story out. He is one example of a CEO who understands how important CNN can be to his company's bottom line. However, not everyone is Sandy Weil, and not everyone is ready for CNN. The right venue could be

Table 5-1   Guidelines for Media Relations on a Smaller Budget

Rely on exclusive relationships with the media to get the word out right– think targeted and high profile!

Get a credible, well-known spokesperson on your side who will generate positive attention for your cause.

Create and promote a knockout media web site to cut costs on production of press materials and, better yet, to reach the international community with great information that's easily accessible.

Skip the press conference. Journalists are hard-pressed to attend so forget it. Better yet, create a web announcement with digital sound bites that can be downloaded from your site.

Generate e-vangelists to spread the word online for you. Provide promotional incentives for your online fans to create buzz and drive traffic to your site.

CNNfn, the financial news channel, for smaller companies, wired or nonwired. Smaller niche cable shows offer great entry points for start-ups. The show will take guests who may not have prominence but represent companies that have an interesting story.

Once an emerging business has attained a certain status, it can in a sense "graduate" to CNN, the *News Hour with Jim Lehrer, Good Morning America*, NBC's *Today*, and other major forums.

Despite the explosion of new publications, both online and offline, and quasireporters who post on message boards and set up home pages, the traditional media has risen to a new level of stature. Media brands have been hard at work building and sustaining their own brands, quite effectively thank you very much. With so many channels and outlets for the consumer eager to obtain news, established daily publications, such as *The New York Times, The San Jose Mercury News, The Washington Post*, and *The San Francisco Chronicle*, have become the leading sources of information nationally and globally. The power of these brands' transcendence online can be seen when we look at how consumers obtain their news today. According to the Pew Internet and American Life Project, one in five Internet users (22 percent) get news online on a typical day, and most of these users go to Internet sites specifically to learn what is in the news. Among those who get news online on a typical day, 55 percent said they went to an Internet news site to read the news, while 43 percent said they happened to see news while they were doing something else online. Even more telling is that the most popular news sites, according to Media Metrix in June 2000, included MSNBC.com, CNN, ABCnews.com, USA Today, as well as WashingtonPost.com and NYTimes.com. MSNBC, the most popular online news site, reported receiving over 4.6 million unique users in the 1-month period.

With so many new publications and online outlets, one might wonder whether consumers and business readers aren't replacing their traditional news sources with online publications and smaller, niche-oriented news sites. In actuality, it appears this abundance of news sources is compelling online news readers to turn to fewer, more established news brands that convey a sense of trust, immediacy, and context with their news stories. A better example couldn't be found than when *The San Antonio Times* reported a mishap at Time Warner's Houston office. The Time Warner executives promised to provide employees with free Road Runner cable service if they ordered first from competitor SBC and then canceled. Unfortunately, this tactic was discovered to be a misguided attempt to gain competitive intelligence. Reuters, AP, and *The New York Times* then reported the story, accompanied by a later story in *The Wall Street Journal* that claimed *The New York Times* broke the story.

Companies recognize and leverage media coverage as an asset. They use it as a foot in the door, as a credibility maker, as the means by which to garner attention from target audiences.

To be sure, there's still room, necessity in fact, for the old-fashioned touch in the wired world. The reality is that trade shows are not going to be made obsolete by e-mail. It is important to fully understand that the digital medium is yet another communications medium, not a replacement for other mediums. Many younger public relations associates don't always understand that concept. They fail to see the importance of going out and establishing personal relationships. Having lunch with a journalist is not part of their mental set. Just a few years ago, young public relations associates were taught from day one that it's important to meet the journalists and try to establish relationships with key media. Now, many of them don't think they need to do it, perhaps brainwashed, to some degree, by other public relations people, who say the value of online communication is that public relations professionals can now avoid the journalists and go directly to the consumer.

But what people forget is that the reason why the journalist is so important is something called journalistic truth, which carries with it huge credibility and is worth enormous sums of money. Yes, the Internet allows you to target consumers directly. There will always be a need for a credible, reliable source to have the ultimate say. That's the role of the journalist, and it's the role of the public relations professional to facilitate the work of that journalist.

Another secret to truly utilizing the power of the media is in the use of online media relations. The Middleberg/Ross Media in Cyberspace study has contributed the largest body of knowledge on how the media work online, a tool that public relations professionals can leverage in campaigns at every opportunity. To be sure, an online-only approach to building awareness and recognition is like a stool with one leg. Solid media relations takes a strong combination of print, broadcast, and online focus to build truly effective communications programs.

However, the power of using the Internet in media relations is one area that has gone untouched, misunderstood, and, at times, treated with fear by some of the leading public relations practitioners of the day. We can begin this discussion by highlighting some key results of the Sixth Annual cyberstudy.

We have been privy to the rapid integration of the Internet into journalists' lives both as investigators and as publishers. Today, three out of four journalists report they go online at least once a day.

Time online is spent researching and using e-mail, as well as downloading digital images. Journalists now use the Internet as frequently and as easily as they use the telephone. (See Figure 5-1.) For the public relations professionals, that means they not

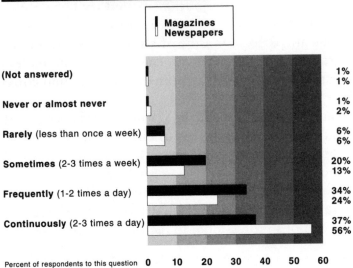

Figure 5-1

only have to understand the space and how it's being used, but they also have to be able to deal with the consequences of its use. If, for example, journalists are picking up misinformation from a rogue site created by a disgruntled employee, the public relations professional has to be web savvy enough to recognize and explain that to the inquirers. He or she must be aware of how to access newsgroups and how to respond to online inquires in a timely and effective manner.

Journalists' use of e-mail has gone through dramatic changes. Usage climbed steadily until 1997 when it reached a plateau and then declined. This backlash can be attributed to the flood of SPAM e-mails to journalists' in boxes. Lisa Napoli, now with MSNBC, reported in 1997 that because her name appeared on a Comdex trade show attendee list, she received over 2000 e-mail messages in addition to the normal, steady flow of useless, whiny, uninformative e-mails she received daily from public relations folks who didn't even know her beat or what types of stories interested her.

The increase observed the following year can be attributed to both an improvement in the use of e-mail by public relations practitioners and the heavy volume of desperate journalists forced to use two and sometimes three e-mail addresses.

The 2000 Middleberg/Ross study revealed that journalists, especially magazine reporters, indicated they had at least two e-mail addresses, one for general releases and one for communications. That's not even counting the one for personal correspondence.

The public relations professional will hopefully have all three of the addresses. But the most vital address to have is the one that the journalist will actually read. That can be crucial at deadline time, or when crisis hit.

E-mail has now become the preferred medium to reach reporters with whom a relationship has been established. (See Figure 5-2.)

In fact, California-based MindArrow Systems has developed e-commercials, a browser application that allows recipients to view multimedia news and information from companies to whom they have given permission.

The system allows a company like Bertelsmann Music Group, for example, to develop new product release videos and background information accessible to journalists, investors, analysts, and others that can be viewed and received within a journalist's e-mail. BMG can not only make more out of their e-mail relationships with this new system but can also track it to see what

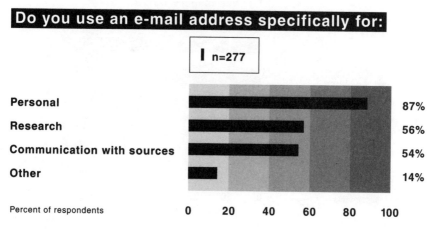

Figure 5-2

information was accessed and the effectiveness of each aspect of their release.

The key is communicating with known journalists in this manner, as e-mail still remains a poor substitute for in-person and over-the-phone introductions. More often than not, unsolicited e-mail, however valuable, is rarely appreciated.

For the first time, the 2000 Middleberg/Ross survey asked journalists if they communicated with readers, and, interestingly, more than half of the journalists surveyed use e-mail with readers at least occasionally. (See Figure 5-3.) That means that journalists are listening ever more closely to the marketplace when considering stories, a valuable piece of information for the public relations professional to leverage.

The use of e-mail by journalists has forced public relations specialists to think of journalism in a new light—it truly is interactive and stories do not "go to bed," as they did in the good old days of pure print. Good journalists will invite discus-

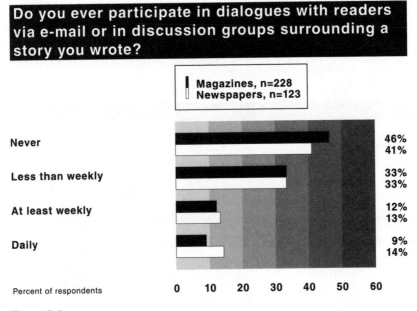

Do you ever participate in dialogues with readers via e-mail or in discussion groups surrounding a story you wrote?

Magazines, n=228
Newspapers, n=123

	Magazines	Newspapers
Never	46%	41%
Less than weekly	33%	33%
At least weekly	12%	13%
Daily	9%	14%

Percent of respondents   0   10   20   30   40   50   60

Figure 5-3

sion and thought through their writing, and many public as well as direct e-mail responses to articles are cropping up to bring completed stories back to the forefront. For example, the Talk Back feature of ZDNet is often fodder for reopening old stories that sparked debate or contained perceived misinformation. Editor Jessie Berst will often revisit an older article in light of new information presented by readers in an online discussion board.

A new development in the Sixth Annual Middleberg/Ross survey looked behind the scenes. In years past, the Middleberg/Ross research focused on nontechnology reporters in order to avoid a skew toward using the Internet, as pretesting had forewarned would occur.

But the most recent study looked at the entire population of journalists, technology and nontechnology. When posttests were conducted on answers aggregated from each population, no significant differences of any kind were discovered.

This finding is quite meaningful because it shows that use of the Internet is just as important for those companies selling perfume as it is for those marketing semiconductors. The rest of the journalist population has completely caught up with the tech-savvy early adopters, making it essential that all public relations executives, across multiple industries, recognize the new ways of working online.

A key trend in the rise of the Internet as a legitimate outlet for news organizations has been the early formation of the online newsroom, which quickly lost its ghetto status and was fully integrated into the traditional newsroom.

The trend is particularly significant for public relations professionals for a number of reasons, but mostly because of the transformation of the speed at which news is now delivered by even the most established media outlets.

Previously, companies were forced to be guided by news cycles and editorial calendars, operational processes that differed in a publications' online and offline editions. For example, *The Wall Street Journal* had a completely separate newsroom.

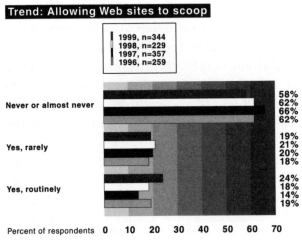

Figure 5-4

Business Week, while it was scooping reporters' print stories for the web site, would run longer, uncut articles online that appeared abridged offline.

Public relations folks were delighted in that they could show their clients that their story had appeared in *Business Week*. (See Figure 5-4.) But that rarely meant as much to them as the print edition that they themselves read.

Today, most businesses are thrilled to appear in the online edition as they have begun to recognize the archival power of the Internet. As of the fall of 1999, 67 percent of newsrooms report that they have been able to integrate their reporting and production so that the flow of information between editors, beats, and reporters is good and growing stronger.

In order to balance the need to keep on the radar screen in a world glutted with news and corporate information, public relations has begun to help companies transform their news production approach.

Rather than advising clients to release only business-critical news, public relations professionals should embrace a "continuous-stream" news cycle with a select push of news to the media.

This means that a company can build and keep awareness and momentum by releasing news and corporate developments, all while realizing that some of these stories will have more archival and investor value than news or feature potential.

Smart companies today are constantly keeping their business partners, potential employees, investors, and evangelists supplied with information, but are more selective about the media onslaught of these news announcements.

It is because of the archival nature of the Internet that this kind of strategy has become effective. Releases that weren't news initially can be magically transformed into news by changing circumstances in the days, weeks, and months following their initial appearance.

Journalists' behavior mirrors that of the public, just as public opinion mirrors journalists. Rarely have journalists reported being interested in audio or video on a corporate site.

However, new evidence supports businesses using new technologies that aid efficiency and connection. Journalists now rely on news tickers on their desktops, personal digital assistants (PDAs), cell phones, and other wireless devices. (See Figure 5-5.)

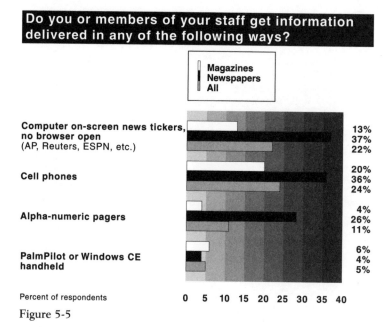

Figure 5-5

Some 6 percent, in fact, use instant messaging on a daily basis. This goes to show that if public relations experts don't consider how to keep up with the device-oriented communications world, they will be neglecting a significant and possibly prominent means of communicating with the media in the future.

Presently, the public relations industry is anticipating an explosion in the use of digital devices. Hopefully, public relations professionals have learned the lesson of e-mail's rise, and will be prepared to take advantage of this new method of contact. Now that we've examined the media's acceleration into the wired world, let's talk about another valuable constituency—the financial and Internet analysts who often shape the media's coverage.

THE NEW STAKEHOLDERS

Stakeholders are those third parties who contribute to the success or failure of a brand. They are both traditional and self-created experts who espouse opinions and analyze and forecast the success of a given company or industry. Before the dawn of the wired world, it was easy to determine who the stakeholders were. It was usually a financial analyst or other market mover, someone prominent in the media, or a prominent consultant whose clout in an industry helped influence opinion. Members of the media are certainly considered one type of brand stakeholders, but these audiences have expanded into less clearly defined categories that include the digerati, celebrities, industry analysts, academics, authors, and political figures among others. It was equally easy to determine who the stakeholder was not; someone without access to the traditional means of conveying information largely relied on word of mouth. While that was sometimes a powerful tool, it rarely translated into status for a particular individual.

Today, that's changed. The advent of the Internet conferred the status of publisher on anyone who has a computer, allowing them, in many cases, to stand shoulder to shoulder with the best that Wall Street has to offer. The Internet is the great equalizer. Text messages from the guy next door who is persistent on various message boards appears on the same computer screen as a quote from General Electric chairman Jack Welch. It's up to the reader to discern the difference. Often, they do not.

Those who are looking to understand how various events have affected the world are constantly searching for context, hoping someone can help them understand new trends and new issues. Part of that audience is the journalist, who turns to analysts for on-the-record confirmations, but uses the third-party influencers on the message boards to gauge the mood of the public at large on certain matters. Often, because of increased deadline pressures on the media, certain third-party influencers and legitimate though less than top-tier analysts can have enormous sway on public opinion. While much of the information disseminated through Internet postings and message boards is believed to be noncredible, some holds weight and continues to sway the opinions and actions of investors, consumers, and journalists alike. The Middleberg/Ross Print Media in Cyberspace study found that 60 percent of journalists responding say they would consider reporting an Internet rumor if confirmed by an independent source. Eight percent of all respondents would consider reporting an unconfirmed Internet rumor. In addition, the media are often caught on tight deadlines, making it impossible to check all information and data found online. Thus, it remains the public relations professional's job to help the journalists find their way to the most authoritative sources of information, while providing a trusted intermediary that can help provide context on messages that may be picked up from the third-party stakeholders.

Among the leaders of the new stakeholders are Internet-centric research firms like Forrester Research of Massachusetts, the Gartner Group of Connecticut, and the recently merged Jupiter Communications and Media Metrix of New York. Each produces high-end research reports on new media developments, runs conferences that are well attended by media and influential industry members, and is often quoted in the major media when an Internet story breaks. In fact, it has been rumored that analysts in these firms receive bonuses based on how much media coverage they generate for their firms. The Internet analyst firms are very important to an overall media relations campaign. Journalists, constantly bombarded with calls about the hottest, newest, best thing since sliced bread, will go to an analyst for a verdict. The analyst will either validate the company and the CEO or turn thumbs down. Therefore, it is incumbent upon the public relations professional to make sure the analyst is totally up to date on the company, and knows about its product and services.

Because of the increased speed of the news cycle wrought by the Internet, public relations specialists work with the industry analyst community much more than the financial analyst community. In fact, very often, financial analysts will depend on the industry analyst, doubling the importance of the validation bestowed by the Jupiters, the Gartners, and the like. Analyst projections and insight have become a standard part of almost every business plan and S-1 filing for the dot-com sector, to the point where many predictions of the billion-dollar markets waiting for sites that sell everything from razor blades to donuts have become almost cliches within the venture capital community.

Projections, of course, often miss their mark, and analyst firms differ greatly in their estimates regarding industry statistics. For example, a poll taken of the analyst firms on how many online shopping carts were abandoned in the 2 weeks prior to Christmas 1999 returned estimates ranging from 8 percent (NYSIA) to 27 percent (Jupiter Communications) to 67 percent (Greenfield Online).

While such projections are accepted with a grain of salt, they remain an integral part of demonstrating market context because they are the best available attempt the industry has at quantifying and understanding what will happen in the future.

Another group of new stakeholders critical to the Internet economy are the venture capitalists and incubator companies who back new businesses. Incubators provide office space, expertise, equipment, and some financial backing in return for a stake in the fledgling companies under their wing. They "incubate" them to a certain point, then release them either to the public market or sell them outright. The concept of the Internet incubator is still relatively new. It caught on rapidly because of the success of such early ventures like CMGI (which actually transformed itself into an incubator after several business incarnations), LC39 (named after a launch pad at Cape

Canaveral), and Idealab of Pasadena, California, led by Bill Gross, the former Knowledge Adventure founder.

A different set of folks who hold influence are the venture capital firms, who gather institutions and individuals in an investment pool that takes stakes in new ventures. While hundreds exist, some of the key players in the sector include Kleiner Perkins, Draper Fisher Jurvetson, Benchmark Capital, Hummer Winblad, and Atlantic. These are the huge, high-profile, top-tier venture capitalists that now rule the roost as Lord Jim once did in his little domain. Their investment decisions make or break companies, as can their actions such as dispensing favors, hiring executives, and getting as involved in business operations as they see fit. Venture capitalists are, in many ways, the allies of public relations. We share the same goals—recognition and financial success for our clients. They appreciate perhaps more than anybody what public relations can do for a company, and insist that the companies they back have not just public relations but also the highest level of public relations. A precondition of many venture capitalists' investments is that a major agency in the field be committed to the project—and it's often the case where the price of that affiliation is of secondary importance.

Getting intellectual capital via public relations is what counts. The cost is not as significant because the results can be so enormous.

For an emerging dot com, acceptance and buy-in by one of these stakeholder audiences can help legitimize the company's business, opening the doors for acceptance by other influencer groups. One example of an idea taking wing because of the caliber of its backers is New York–based InfoRocket.com. The company launched the world's first question-and-answer marketplace powered by a person-to-person auction in January 2000. This was a revolutionary idea, quickly connecting people with questions to people with answers—for a price—with InfoRocket.com conducting the transaction. It soon became clear that while the model was compelling, it was littered with many uncertainties, including problems with copyright, veracity, consumer protection, and fraud. In addition, the jury was still out as to whether or not a one-to-one or peer-to-peer advice site could make any money on the Internet or would just simply compliment more profitable Internet business directories. User traffic was another limiting factor. Without enough visitors volunteering their expertise, InfoRocket.com would be no better than the average search engine, albeit one with a cost attached.

But InfoRocket.com was financed by a blue chip panel of investors from Draper Fisher Jurvetson, and had the blessing from key media influencer and Garage.com founder Guy Kawasaki. That pedigree helped the company attract top talent, including a high-profile CEO, garner media attention, and gain the sage advice of industry experts, all combining to help build a tight growth strategy. InfoRocket.com closed a second round of venture capital funding in April 2000 worth approximately $25 million that was led by the highly touted firm of The Carlyle Group. This financial backing, coming from a well-respected, high-profile venture capital firm, established InfoRocket.com as a major player in the eyes of the investment community. Any previous doubts about the business model or potential legalities that InfoRocket.com could face were put on hold.

The rest will be up to InfoRocket.com.

One of the keys to the emerging dot-com universe is the people who largely control investor perception of how a company is doing.

These people are the financial analysts, the titans of Olympus, the people whose views can move markets. Today, media relations access to the great analysts is extremely difficult. Analyst meetings are extremely difficult, if not impossible, to hold. Analysts are now stars, godlike market shakers who won't take phone calls. People like Ralph Acumopura, who runs research for Prudential, or Mary Meeker of Morgan-Stanley, an acclaimed Internet analyst, or Henry Blodgett of Merrill Lynch, earn salaries that are equal to, if not bigger than, the dot-com officials they report on.

As a result of the growing importance of the analyst community, truly objective research is particularly hard to find. Analysts are often asked to act as quasiinvestment bankers. In fact, it is rare to see a negative report produced by an analyst whose firm is the underwriter of the company he or she is covering. More times than not, that analyst was, in good part, responsible for that company going to his or her firm in the first place. That's because the analyst has taken on new roles as an investment banker, and the analyst, in many ways, is responsible for attracting much of the investment banking business to the firm. So the analyst is compelled to put out reports on companies in which the firm has a financial stake. Roughly, about 80 percent of analyst calls are buy recommendations. Selling a stock may be good advice, but conservative financial postures are currently out of vogue on Wall Street.

It was a lot easier to reach analysts back in the good old days of the 1970s. Public relations specialists used to gather them together by holding what was called an "analyst lunch," which really meant that a secretary would get on the phone, call these folks, and see if they would like to attend a free lunch. Very often, that's all it took, a nice, free lunch with plenty of booze at Wall Street's Harry's Bar or, before Harry's, Delmonico's on Beaver Street in the heart of New York's financial district. The financial analysts got together, there was a presentation, and then those that were turned on would usually issue a buy recommendation or some type of research report within 24 hours. It was just that easy.

There were other techniques that used to reach market movers. When it came time for an earnings report, it was not uncommon to issue a press release that would go to the same five key news outlets—*The New York Times*, *The Wall Street Journal*, Associated Press, Reuters, and then usually one local outlet. If the company was based in Des Moines, it was *The Des Moines Register*. If it was in Los Angeles, it was *The Los Angeles Times*.

That was considered adequate distribution. Occasionally, public relations specialists would became even more creative and did something called the Dow Joneser, which involved offering an exclusive to a Dow Jones reporter. Public relations people would tip the journal reporter to what the earnings were expected to be, which today is referred to as the "whisper number," or the likely direction the company will go rather than the earlier estimates of earnings that securities law requires them to issue. Armed with that information, a story would appear in *The Wall Street Journal* on the day the earnings were officially released, describing what the earnings were to be and what the outlook was for the company as seen by the chairperson. Back in those days, the game was severely weighted in favor of the privileged insiders. Institutional investors almost always got all the inside information way before the public, having been tapped in to the analysts who attended the Harry's lunches. In some cases, institutional investors themselves were often invited to these lunches, but the little guy was absolutely shut out.

Presently, the tables are turning in favor of the individual investor. Thanks to pressure from the Securities and Exchange Commission (SEC) and the rise of the Internet, the little guy is now receiving information on a more timely basis. They still are not quite on the same level as the institutional investor, but they can come closer to it than ever before. The analyst meeting at Harry's is now being replaced by the analyst call, literally phone calls, often accessible via the Internet, where analysts listen to the chairperson of a company and ask questions. Those calls are now being broadcast online and the individual investors are being invited to attend. Thus, they get the information at the same time as the institutional analyst. As a corollary to that change, the nature and importance of investor relations has changed dramatically. Internet communications and other forms of direct communication with investors can be more efficient channels to build relationships with a more empowered investment audience than limiting relationships to the financial analyst community.

The Internet has also spawned a new treasure chest of informational riches. There are companies that specialize in ways to help the individual investor. Multex.com is a company that will send investors, for a charge, analyst reports from Goldman, First Boston, Merrill Lynch, and others. They, in effect, aggregate these reports and then distribute them to anyone who is willing to pay a fee. That allows individual investors to have access to the same kinds of in-depth research as the institutional investor, a major change. Today, the investor is the consumer, rather than some gray eminence residing exclusively in the towers of Wall Street. And, oft times, investor relations is better understood and undertaken under the guise of a marketing effort rather than courting relationships with a walled community.

While the industry analyst community has become a defining factor in many Internet company success stories, the praise must be across the board. The favorable view and backing by one group of analysts, no matter how prominent, does not guarantee a consensus among all analysts, nor does it guarantee that the individual investor understands or supports the product. Such was the case for a premier provider of e-business building and marketing services that experienced the ups and downs of analysis. We'll call this company EBuildingBlocks.com in deference to its sensitive history in the marketplace. Initially, EBuildingBlocks.com was embraced by financial analysts as a company with tremendous growth capability, a compelling financial model, and a truly unique service offering. Many financial analysts who reviewed the company's prospects recommended the stock as a strong buy.

This praise, however, was largely contained within the financial analyst community. Media coverage remained limited and highly focused among certain industry sectors, leaving investors somewhat skeptical in light of the financial community endorsement. If this company was so great and so likely for success, they reasoned, how come no one was writing about it? The reasons behind this divergence can be attributed to confusion and lack of understanding regarding both the company and the undefined market space they were entering.

EBuildingBlocks.com separates itself from direct marketers by touting itself as a commerce enabler, a company focused on building long-term customer value when companies engaged in its relationship building programs, either online or offline.

Unfortunately, its public relations efforts were unable to point out the differences between EBuildingBlocks.com and its competitors. The public relations team could not leverage the understanding by the financial community into tangible communications and education of the media and the industry analysts.

EBuildingBlocks.com wasn't devastated by the media's disconnect, but its growth was undoubtedly slowed. It went on to prove the power of its technology platform and a patented business process through its branded network in more than the financial community.

It eventually evolved as a provider of infrastructure solutions to serve as the "arms dealer" to help businesses optimize their customer relationships through the use of loyalty and related programs.

Their ongoing challenge, however, remained the same: continue to educate as well as innovate.

One audience is not enough anymore. The winners are those that create a network of digerati and industry influencers who can help a business build a cushion of third-party support.

Unless emerging and traditional companies expand the horizons of influencers with which they are building relationships, it is likely even the biggest brands will fall from grace with the influencers.

Even more interesting, and possibly frightening, than those analysts who work for professional companies and have reputations that are backed by years of credentials and solid research are the "analysts" that are further down the food chain—the so-called online insiders. Because of the anonymity of the Internet, gossip can be couched as expertise. Many online messengers have no credentials outside of self-conferred know-how, yet deliver their messages with a ring of authority. Generally, most commentators of this ilk are merely people who make comments on Internet financial talk sites such as Raging Bull.com, Silicon Investor, or Yahoo! Investor. These are people who are likely amateurs, but who are very important amateurs who voice their opinions about the value and the prospects of Internet stocks.

Many of them claim to have insider knowledge, but there is often little evidence to back their claims. Many of them specialize in volatile rumors and overhead tales, many of them actionable. Yet it would be wrong to underestimate their influence. Like advertising, an online analyst's constant repetition confers a message and makes an impression. And, in fact, some of them become quite well known in the mainstream. The Motley Fool, started by the Gardner Brothers as an Internet chat group, blossomed into a highly trafficked site, a syndicated radio show, and a multimillion-dollar business. But the essence of what they did came from the online world, giving them a forum for their particular expertise, financial stocks. Today, many sites offer users the ability to rank the opinions and advice disseminated by an online persona.

A peculiar subspecies of this informal group of new stakeholders is the *day trader*, people who hold no long-term position in a stock, but trade in and out of many, sometimes within minutes, hoping to eke out a small profit. The day trader has largely built an entire new industry, the online broker. Without the day trader, there would be no AmeriTrade, E-Trade, or Datek. Those companies survive because of the activities and commissions generated by the day trader, and there are probably a hundred other companies equally dependent on them.

The day traders are very difficult to control. Obviously, they chat among themselves on Yahoo! investment forum to Raging Bull and Silicon Alley Investor. Such chatter often does more harm than good, and certain messages of imminent disaster— usually unfounded—can do quite a bit of damage to a stock's price by spreading rumor or incorrect information. Companies, and particularly their public relations teams, must now monitor what the day traders are saying online, if only to protect themselves from false information or information that isn't timely. This audience must be treated quite differently than the very public personas of the industry and financial analysts, venture capitalists, and other digerati. Any hesitation in reacting to them merely provides fodder for additional piling on by other so-called experts, leading to a consensus building of uninformed speculation that could potentially sway a serious tastemaker or news outlet.

Another subset of the day trader is the *short seller*. These are people who sell stocks in anticipation of the stock declining. There have been a number of cases where short sellers have spread false information online to the detriment of companies' revenue, stock price, and employee acquisition. One example is a company called PressTek. A New York Stock Exchange Company, PressTek's stock suddenly started tumbling one day for no apparent reason. Eventually, the chairman of that company told *The Wall Street Journal* that he traced the decline to false information spread by short sellers about how the company was doing.

A more interesting case is a company that makes zinc-coated throat lozenges. ABC's *20/20* did a very positive piece on the effectiveness of the zinc lozenges, in particular one brand. The stock of that lucky brand started to zoom upward shortly thereafter. But suddenly, fortunes reversed, and it started heading down. The company was bewildered at the downturn until they started looking into the situation. They found that, once again, short sellers were spreading false information online, going so far as to create a false press release, which was even carried on the Bloomberg financial wire. Yet, these early bell-weather stories have yet to do much for companies looking to the SEC or outside parties to protect them online. By the time most companies are able to garner legal counsel or action toward online naysayers, it is often too late. (See Table 6-1.)

For example, an online insider board known as "The Truthseeker" has been sued by ZiaSun Technologies for promoting misinformation among posters. Their lawsuit could extend for months. Meanwhile, information on ZiaSun circulates around the Internet, creating not only a legal issue but also a massive communications problem that must be handled faster than subpoenas and court orders allow. The lesson here for communicators is that legal recourse must be coupled with responsive communications. Companies must post and release accurate, corrective information when necessary, make relevant parties aware of the misinformation, and ensure the rumor does not reemerge to cause further damage. Unfortunately, no company is safe from this set of rumormongering stakeholders. Lucent Technologies became a victim of short sellers when a fake news release designed to look as if it came from the company was posted on a Yahoo! message warning of a profit shortfall in the second quarter. The posting briefly knocked the company's shares down 3.6 percent before Lucent moved to expose the scheme.

Table 6-1   Do's and Don'ts for Building Relationships with the Online Insiders

Do's	Don'ts
Create a special e-communique for your online audience with some information not available elsewhere to make it valuable and attractive.	Don't blast e-mail a standard press release to the online community and/or post in newsgroups. This will be unappreciated and most likely, ignored.
Do encourage the online audience to forward information to their friends and colleagues–better yet, ask them to refer others to your web site for more information.	Don't relegate handling an online rumor to your legal team only. Involve other internal image stake-holders, such as customer service representatives, media and investor relations, compliance officers, and human resources.
Do notify the SEC and other third parties if you become aware of inaccurate information circulating on the Internet about your company.	Don't permit employees to respond directly to miscellaneous rumors and hearsay they uncover on the Internet. Negative and inaccurate postings and sites should be handled in a centralized fashion, not unlike a media inquiry.
Encourage feedback on your web site from the online community and most importantly, *respond quickly.* No one appreciates being ignored.	Don't forget that you may have as many, if not more, "friends" than "foes" in the online chat rooms and message boards.

These horror stories are rampant—nearly every company has faced some kind of scare from the persuasive force of the online insiders. The boards that display these postings have fluctuated in their policies regarding taking down inaccuracies. Most defend the right to free speech, and one trend to watch is a growing reluctance for message boards to provide identifying information on posters to official inquiries. America Online and the Microsoft Network allow posters 2 weeks to respond to a subpoena for their identifying information prior to releasing it to authorities, all in accordance with the growing number of revised standards and practices in online privacy.

*   *   *

How do you win in this new stakeholder world? How do you differentiate yourself? How does your company build and maintain these relationships with this new set of influencers? Obviously, it's important to start catering to the industry analyst. Public relations professionals need to meet on a regular basis with the Jupiters and the Forresters and the Gartners of the world, make a presentation, and get them on board for their companies. The problem, as with the financial analysts mentioned earlier, is that these analysts may cover a company, but they won't go to any great lengths unless the company is a client of the industry analyst.

It's not particularly easy to be a client, either. It can cost a company well over six figures to be a client, get exposure in analyst reports, and be able to attend conferences.

But the industry analyst obviously has to be worked in order to cut through the clutter of numerous businesses vying for attention, so many companies pay the price. Often, it's the price of success. As we've seen, the media and analysts have enormously speeded up the way a story migrates to the rest of the world. Sometimes, that can lead to problems. Let's examine some of the ways a crisis can occur, and how savvy public relations professionals can control them once they hit.

THE CEO AS CELEBRITY

Today, being named CEO of a dot com has become a status symbol unlike anything ever afforded corporate executives in the traditional age of business. It also carries public relations pressure usually seen in traditional business only during a crisis period.

Because technology stocks are volatile, CEOs spend a lot of time on the hot seat, their every pronouncement carrying great implications for entire sectors of the market. This is particularly noticeable since the great dot-com crash of April, 2000. Now that the bloom is off the rose, technology CEOs must put even greater emphasis on their company's public relations. One wrong move in the highly scrutinized technology sector could prove disastrous. Thus, the need for great media training supervised by public relations professionals has never been greater.

But such pressure also carries great rewards. Perhaps because the companies they lead now command market capitalizations surpassing industrial age giants, the Internet leaders have become major celebrities in their own right, their faces peering out from magazine covers, their comments debated on news shows, their keynote addresses filling convention halls.

The challenge for public relations professionals is pairing the experiential assets of these sometimes seasoned executives with the Internet industry issues and categories they can own. It's no accident that some CEOs are quoted more than others. Besides the valiant efforts of their public relations counselor, the CEO who gets press is often the most journalist friendly. The prime requirement to reach that exalted status is simple: the journalist must know that when the CEO is called, the CEO will take the call and will answer inquiries fully and completely. Journalists are usually on extraordinarily tight schedules. They can't afford to have someone say, "I'll get back to you in 2 hours." Those who take the call—people like Jeff Bezos of Amazon and Kim Polese of Marimba—inevitably will make the news. It saves journalists time and hassle.

Today, the public demands not only that the Internet CEOs run a fast, profitable company but also that they demonstrate charisma, charm, and savvy. For an Internet CEO is the company personified like never before. Many new business initiatives and the introduction of new technologies require the education of the consumer and business audience. This, in turn, leads to endorsement and support of a new product or service. Thus, the CEO must be this market educator.

Ironically, the best leaders often generate so much support for a new category that they pave the way for other competitors to enter the space and be successful. For example, Michael Dell has long represented the face of customized buying to order and has continuously pushed the envelope for how personalized purchasing can transform the experience brand. Dell has, however, created such fascination and acceptance for this model that companies like General Motors are citing Dell's accomplishments as the reason they, too, are embarking on a similar strategy.

But public relations professionals blessed with a charismatic CEO can't just sit back and let the magic flow. They must work to broaden the executive's constituency beyond the immediate company. It's a tactic that will ultimately boost not only the company but also the market sector, an equally important factor in obtaining investor respect. The way to achieve that goal is to position CEOs as diplomatic representatives of the particular niche they're in. They speak not only for their company but also for the category, be it e-commerce, privacy, or streaming audio and video software. Many CEOs have already achieved such status. For example, Scott Kurnit from About.com has successfully defined himself as the quintessential smart, very quick, but tough Internet businessman. Darian Dash from Digital Mafia, a company that develops web business strategies and sites for black-owned businesses and organizations, has made himself an oft-cited representative for minority-owned Internet business discussions. Kevin O'Connor of DoubleClick is one of the people media turn to for quotes on Internet advertising and marketing.

In the Internet sector, the authority to develop into that sort of spokesperson usually goes to the first charismatic person who seizes the high ground and claims ownership of a new or emerging category. If a company is fast enough to be first to market, it can establish the market category and its perceptual association with that category will grow with the market. Of course, such leadership can also present problems. No one wants to answer questions about negative issues in the category if they're not peculiar to their own particular business. But it comes with the turf, and usually, a great spokesperson can spin the issue so as to reflect great credit on his or her own company, while minimizing the impact on their own business. Great examples include Jeff Bezos' take on Amazon's one-click patents or Bill Gates' staunch defense of Microsoft's right to excel.

While CEOs of emerging Internet brands are all carving new ground, it takes a special kind of authority to become identified with a category. Not every CEO has it, and few recognize that they don't. Some CEOs are excellent at carrying out a message for the industry rather than their particular company. In particular, the high-tech CEOs are masters at it. Larry Ellison at Oracle, Scott McNealy from Sun, and Andy Grove at Intel were able to be excellent spokespeople for an industry that consumers wanted to know more and more about. Ideally, the Internet business community thinks of the CEO and then thinks of the company simultaneously, a perfect branding opportunity to gain awareness and the attention of the marketplace. It is the job of the public relations professional to encourage those who may not realize their talents, and certainly to be very diplomatic in letting other chiefs know that their skills are best suited to other areas of company operations.

The best way to create a larger awareness for a company is to make the CEO the educator and standard setter for the category. This is a role that cannot be filled by a celebrity or other evangelist. They carry too much baggage from their other endeavors, and while that may be highly appropriate for advertising situations, it is not the way to project a serious image for an emerging company. It needs to establish its own reputation. (See Table 7-1.) With the CEO as celebrity, it is much easier to deal with media and offer them an expert, thus making for a better story. Larry Kramer, the CEO of CBS MarketWatch, is a great example of a company leader who managed to seize the high ground from competitors despite a late entry into the field. Although CBS MarketWatch launched with an incredible brand name, there was little awareness of the site in the early going. CBS had not yet made a significant move to the web or in financial news, and essentially had to start from scratch. The task was daunting, as successful players like Yahoo! CNNfn, CNBC, and Motley Fool were already moving into the space.

Choosing to profile Larry Kramer was an easy decision with his strong journalism background and stellar reputation among his media colleagues. Among his many accomplishments, Kramer had been editor at the *San Francisco Examiner* and metro editor at *The Washington Post*. Before joining CBS Marketwatch, Kramer had initiated a highly successful information delivery service for sports scores, a precursor to the Palm Pilot, at DBC.

CBS Marketwatch quickly established a reputation for quality news and production, but still struggled for attention in the early going. Through an equity deal with parent company CBS, the financial site garnered cross-medium exposure and Kramer appeared regularly on the CBS Marketwatch minute introduced by Dan Rather on the evening news. The turning point came in January 1999, when the company scored one of the most successful IPOs in Wall Street history. That gave the site new momentum, and Kramer was ready to seize the day. The IPO validated his position in the market, and his savvy public relations team quickly positioned him as an expert source in the dynamic world of online journalism.

The Internet and financial news were the perfect marriage, Kramer proclaimed, and represented the future of journalism. As an ex print journalist and now successful Internet entrepreneur, Kramer had the authority to make such bold claims. Media reporter Felicity Barringer said Kramer had "visited all the signs of the cross of journalism." Now, it was time to take advantage of that stature. His public relations team began pitching him as both journalist and businessman, a unique hybrid capable of straddling the delicate line between church and state that is always drawn in newsrooms. Kramer was positioned against several other high-profile journalist/businessmen who had been causing a stir in the market. One of the most popular—mainly for its catchy hook—was pitting his market position against James Cramer of TheStreet.com. It was Kramer vs. Cramer, and the press ate it up. Off screen, the two were actually friends. It didn't hurt that Larry Kramer was an articulate and passionate spokesman for this new wave of journalism. He was sent on numerous media tours, and acquitted himself well in the give and take of these sessions. At the end of that phase of his campaign, Larry Kramer had built enormous credibility as a spokesman for high-quality, instantaneous financial journalism on the Internet. He owned the category, establishing his edge against his competitors. When CBS MarketWatch was mentioned, Larry Kramer came immediately to mind. It was the perfect marriage of the CEO as celebrity with a business concept in need of attention. CBS MarketWatch.com rose to become the most popular financial news site as ranked by Media Metrix and continues to be in the top 10 most visited news sites on a regular basis.

An analogy can be made that a spokesperson is to a CEO what advertising is to public relations. A CEO needs to provide business context and credibility to an operation. They are the voice of the serious side of the business, the person who leads her or his company through the thorny issues of the business world. On the other hand, a spokesperson attracts attention and awareness, drawing new potential customers into the circus

Table 7-1   Does Your CEO Have What it Takes to Build a Brand in the New Economy?

Is he/she willing to take an alternative or not popular point of view?

Can he/she provide insider perspective? If not, can he/she leverage outsider perspective?

Does he/she personify the brand?

Does he/she spend significant time with all stakeholders, including employees, media and customers, and not just investors?

Does he/she use the Internet, cell phones, and PDAs? Can he/she relate from personal experience to the consumer changes in the Internet economy?

Does he/she have the internal support from key executives to maintain a leadership role in the public eye during times of change?

Does he/she appear credible, believable, and trustworthy?

Does he/she speak the language of the today's business?

tent to take a look at the company's offerings. The classic example of the last few years has been Priceline.com's use of William Shatner. Although Priceline.com's CEO Jay Walker is an amazing public speaker and evangelist for his particular niche on the Internet, name-your-own-price sales, it's clear that the company would not have attracted nearly as much attention as it has if it had not decided to use Shatner as its spokesperson. Shatner, of course, was beloved to TV and film audiences as the intrepid Captain James T. Kirk, the leader of the U.S.S. *Enterprise*. He was a space pioneer who boldly led one of the biggest cult television shows ever, but Shatner also had credibility as someone who understood that he was merely an actor in the space drama, and had a respected sense of humor about his typecasting in the role. Enter Priceline. The upstart Internet company had a war chest for a celebrity, but offered a greater inducement—stock options. Shatner was willing to take a shot, and advertising history was born. Today, Priceline and Shatner are virtually viewed by the public as one and the same. But Walker has also maintained a strong role as the spokesperson for the business side of the operation, a tricky balance, but one he has carried well.

Despite Shatner's icon status and the great reception for his television commercials, investors and the financial community would be beaming out of the stock were Shatner left to handle the sometimes nuanced speech necessary when explaining a company's position in the market.

During the launch of Priceline's Webhouse Club, Walker didn't blink an eye when asked to drive 2 hours for a 15-minute media interview with a medium-profile industry trade publication. He understood: public relations has been kind to brands like Priceline, and it is no secret that Walker has made himself a true friend to the media. In doing so, Walker has been able to claim rights to becoming the "alternate" spokesperson for online travel, grocery, and mortgage business. Priceline, in turn, has successfully positioned itself as the "other" within its own category, with immediate top-of-mind differentiation from other online travel and lifestyle competitors. In general, celebrity spokespeople create publicity that can be leveraged into news stories that explore the more serious side of a business. They also help create momentum for a company, serving almost as a stamp of approval, or tacit nod that an older company "gets it" when it comes to a particular space. One of the fringe benefits of having a celebrity spokesperson is that everyone wants to meet her or him. Obtaining meetings for venture capitalists and other investors is a lot easier if there's a familiar star aboard willing to shake hands for an hour.

Sometimes, a CEO becomes an accidental spokesperson for a category, rising to the top by his or her sheer willingness to take on tough issues and present him or herself as the alternative to the establishment. No better example of that exists than MP3.com, the online music site, and its CEO Michael Robertson. Robertson began MP3.com out of his bedroom in a San Diego, California, suburb. Already a veteran of several business start-ups and one failure, Robertson was in his early 30s and absolutely fearless. He would prove to be the perfect spokesperson for the emerging category of music downloads. Having purchased the key URL MP3.com from an Internet entrepreneur for $1000, Robertson set about establishing himself as an expert in the Internet music sector by writing an online column, "Michael's Minute." The archives of those columns quickly became a resource for fans, journalists, and music industry executives seeking to get up to speed on the issues surrounding the digital distribution of music.

What Robertson brought to the table was an outsider's perspective. Several of his more inflammatory quotes made national publications take notice of his operation and, soon, he was being regularly quoted whenever an opposing viewpoint to the record industry was needed. The attention soon paid off. When Robertson's company went public in July 1999, its first-day share price proved to be one of the year's hottest IPOs, temporarily creating a company whose market capitalization rivaled that of the major music distributors.

The public good will generated by a CEO as a spokesperson for his or her company and category is never more necessary than in times of crisis.

After bidding on eBay was halted for 22 hours in June 1999—only the third site shutdown in the company's history—CEO Meg Whitman showed corporate ownership and commitment when she stepped forward and took full responsibility for the problems that had plagued her site. Whitman refused to leave the office during the weekend until the cause of the outage was identified. She sincerely apologized to the millions of customers, and was never defensive about the reasons for the shutdown. Whitman told the *Dallas Morning News* that the company had "taken a serious look at our priorities because of this outage. . . .We hope you will give us the chance to show you our commitment to your success and to keeping eBay up and running 24 hours, 7 days a week." Two days later, in the European edition of *The Wall Street Journal*, Whitman was even more contrite. "We can't apologize enough for this disruption," she said. "We want to earn back your trust." All of this came in the face of news that revenue losses could be as high as $2 million.

But Whitman gave consumers and business audiences exactly what they were starving for: honesty, commitment, and humility.

Table 7-2 How to Shepherd Your Company Through a Crisis on the Internet Successfully

---

Be willing to participate in online forums. Consider even holding your own online town hall.

Don't overreact to information found on the Internet—true or untrue.

Consider setting aside a special area of your web site for business partners alongside that for media and consumers.

Provide public statements online and update them regularly on your web site.

Ensure privacy and security are of utmost importance in online crisis communications.

Recognize global linguistic and cultural implications of communicating on the web.

Embody the feelings of concern and empathy for those affected by your company's crisis.

Don't be defensive. Acknowledge shortcomings and mistakes—be forthcoming with known information.

Whitman had astutely sensed the moment in time, and had reacted appropriately. The public and the news media had been inundated with stories of Internet businesses that could seemingly do no wrong. They were very eager to slap back about poor customer service.

Yet, eBay took the blows and ultimately bought back the loyalty and consumer commitment and community they had worked so hard to craft and competitors envied. (See Table 7-2.)

There are times when no public relations can top the sheer charisma some CEOs bring to their jobs. It's time to stand back and get out of the way. Bob Lessin was vice chairman of investment banking at Smith Barney when Andy Klein was starting up the first online investment bank that allowed individual investors access to IPOs. Two years later, in 1998, Lessin left to join Wit Soundview Technologies, formerly Wit Capital, and transformed himself into the ubersalesperson of New York's Silicon Alley. Picture this former vice chairman of Smith Barney, one of Wall Street's top executives, coming out of his box-filled, computer-strewn office in a golf shirt, khakis that would make The Gap proud, and socks with holes in both of the big toes.

He also had a big smile, phones ringing off of the hook, and conducted his no-nonsense business in 18 minutes. That played well with the media, and generated a significant number of stories about Lessin's transformation. But even more crucial to the story was what he actually did when he arrived at Wit. When Lessin came aboard, he brought it instant credibility as a "real" investment bank. He also made deals flow, steering Wit into 176 IPOs in 1999. Both his reputation and contacts helped bring Wit to the next level. With over 20 years of experience on Wall Street, Lessin filled the investment bank with similarly seasoned Wall Street professionals, such as Jonathan Cohen, who had been vice chairman of Charles Schwab. It was that level of credibility that made the public relations machine's job easier.

Soon, online IPO access and Wit Soundview became synonymous. It wasn't necessarily because of the media coverage. It was the what the CEO already had on his resume.

There are secrets to getting the CEO to understand the difference between speaking for his or her company and speaking for the category.

Hiring outside trainers, media specialists, who provide extensive lists of questions and answers, is one option commonly used. These trainers, often former members of the television media, teach an executive the subtle nuances that come across on camera, reminding them that the slightest inappropriate gesture can ruin the crux of the message. Remember Richard Nixon in the 1960 televised presidential debates? Nixon may have lost that election because of public perceptions that he looked haggard and evasive. Similarly, a random scratch of the nose, darting eyes, or tilt of the head at key moments can obliterate a CEO's on-camera image, turning the story into one about the messenger rather than the message.

Smart public relations counselors will require the CEO for new clients to undergo media training. It's simply that crucial to success. A CEO must be able to think on his or her feet as fast as any movie star in an action film.

Public relations professionals must be aware of what can go wrong in any given situation in order to be able to react in a proper fashion. Let me share a story with you that illustrates what can go wrong. Dan Kadlec is a well-respected financial writer whose column currently appears in *Time* magazine. Earlier, Dan's work appeared in *USA Today*. At that time, in order to build a relationship between him and one particular financial analyst, we set up a meeting so that they could get to know each other and share some views.

The analyst wins by gaining exposure. Dan gets a new source and possibly some news. As is typical of those sessions, Dan's first question was something along the lines of, "So, what stocks do you like?" It's a bridge-building question. It's an easy opener, and it draws out the knowledge of the analyst. He can direct the conversation wherever he wants. Most surprisingly, the analyst said, "I like a lot, but I can't tell you any of them on the record." Dan looked around and asked, "So, why are we here?"

The lesson from that session is that the journalist is really the client, and public relations professionals have to have both sides of the conversation fully prepped prior to any meeting. Having a prior relationship with Dan prevented that meeting from being a total disaster, but it could have been. But a public relations professional cannot afford to lose a Dan Kadlec as a contact. Losing a client, yes. Losing Dan Kadlec, that's a major no-no.

Media training today is much more sophisticated than it was even a few years ago. The video crews that tape sessions now consist of several members, and are usually fronted by a highly experienced interviewer. A key to the entire session is to put the CEO through a rigorous Q&A session. He or she must be asked every difficult, obnoxious question that someone could ask. Anything less will catch up to the CEO at some point because today's media is highly aggressive, and there are many more outlets all competing for the same story. Thus, the gloves must come off.

Like a professional magician, the media-trained CEO learns the subtle art of misdirection. They take a question and send the answer off in a direction that does not head to the heart of the answer. It's not lying. And it's not really being that evasive. It's somewhat nonresponsive, but it is an answer. And the best CEOs can deliver it with such charm that all but the most tenacious journalists will be disinclined to pursue the point with follow-up questions. For example, a typical tough question might be, "Mr. Jones, I understand you have an acquisition ready to announce next week. What is it?" The worst possible response would be to say, "No comment." That would indicate there is a deal, and could lead to wild media speculation, not the best thing for a company's image.

The ideal way to deflect that question is with a broader statement. "We are constantly looking at deals. We are constantly in different stages of negotiation with a wide variety of companies, and as soon as a deal is ready to be announced, you'll be the first to know."

The answer leaves open the possibility that there may be an acquisition. It also leaves open the possibility that there may not be an acquisition. It also ensures the journalist that he or she is in the loop should an acquisition occur. In short, it covers the bases. Another possible question, slightly testier, might be, "Mr. Jones, we understand that you are being sued by a former secretary for sexual harassment. Is that true?"

Mr. Jones could go in several different directions, depending on the circumstances. Certainly, the way to respond if it's not true is to emphatically deny it. But if it is true, a better answer might be, "that's the kind of question that is appropriate in this kind of situation, and I choose to respond." There's no denial. There's merely a Fifth Amendment sort of response, which leaves the question open for another day, when perhaps a fuller explanation may be in order. Another way to take on a tough question is to use it as the basis for an affirmation of your position on another issue. "Mr. Jones, you have a major new product whose sales are way below expectations. I understand there's an exposé that will be released tomorrow on your company. Is it true?"

That's where the savvy CEO will take the bull by the horns. The proper response? "I'm glad you brought that up." That opening allows the answer to be turned into a positive statement on the situation. It shows that you're willing to defend your position and gives the impression of candor.

*   *   *

It's extraordinary how many things do come out when viewed on videotape. Such subtle things as speech patterns, hesitations, slurs, all bloom like roses on the tape. Another crucial aspect of preparing your CEO is the notion of how to respond to difficult questions. Politicians are masters at that last item. The senator from Utah, Orrin Hatch, is a particular genius at it. The media can ask him a question, and he immediately turns his response around to reflect a new spin. It's like someone never asked him the question. He answers in his own way. It's a true talent, but it's something that can be taught. It all comes from practice, and that's where media training comes in. The more time the CEO puts into training, the less sweat when confronted.

Before a CEO sits down with a member of the media, whether it's print or broadcast or even online, that CEO should be thoroughly prepped on every conceivable difficult question that could be raised, and given suggestions on how to respond. No journalist should win the Pulitzer Prize at the CEO's expense. That said, it is not recommended that CEOs put themselves in a position to respond to breaking news without preparation. If at all possible, media interviews should be formally structured and set up. There are other spokespeople who can handle the initial wave in a crisis. As the ultimate leader, the CEO must provide the final answer.

One question public relations professionals should be sure to ask prospective clients is "How available will your CEO be to entertain questions and in-person interviews with the media?" Without executive commitment to media and overall public relations, a company is likely not to be able to gain the kind of momentum necessary to make headway in a market. The lack of commitment to media relations may also be a sign that the company ultimately does not understand what public relations can do for them. And those are companies that are musts to avoid for any serious public relations professional.

Who is the quintessential CEO celebrity? Is it Steve Case, Gerald Levin, Carly Fiorina? The answer lies in that qualities of a great CEO are somewhat the same, but can be translated in different ways. Ideally, the CEO has to maintain an image somewhere between Microsoft's Bill Gates and Oracle's Larry Ellison. Gates, before his post antitrust ruling attempts at warming himself up, formerly came across as dry, geeky, and self-centered. On the other side of the spectrum, Oracle's Ellison is over the top, almost the image of a cartoon politician in the way he carries himself. He lives life out loud, letting his public persona as somewhat of a playboy mesh with his job as a business leader. In between those two extremes is a happy medium, embodied by several successful CEOs. Marimba CEO Kim Polese has refined media schmoozing to an art form. She's very accessible and able to explain what new technology can do for consumers and businesses without being condescending. She's also very educated on the big-picture issues, and has a human quality rare in Internet CEOs. Broadcom CEO Henry Nicholas embodies the passion and drive that all CEOs need. Nicholas is akin to rock singer Henry Rollins in his relentless approach to life and business. He's been known to hire a personal trainer for a midnight to 3 a.m. session after one of his typical 18-hour workdays, and he's widely credited with infusing that focus into his staff at Broadcom.

Internet savvy is best associated with GE chairman Jack Welch, who wasn't too proud to admit that he had to hire his own coach to bring himself up to speed on the Internet. Yet, he's been able to turn around perceptions that he's out of the loop on the topic, and has brought himself and his company quickly up to speed. Patience, a critical trait in top CEOs, is exemplified by IBM's Jim Corgel. He's leading the company's efforts to explore the "Net Generation" business, which reaches out to small business and start-ups, not the traditional IBM target market. Corgel is not trying to change Big Blue in a day, but realizes that patience and persistence will pay off. Finally, Yahoo!'s Jerry Yang practices what he preaches, creating a public persona that matches the consumer perception of his company, something every CEO strives to duplicate. Yang is fun, smart, capable of being a little bit wacky, exuding youth and fun.

He's exactly what people want from the head of a company with the unusual name of Yahoo!

Great Internet CEOs will embody some of these characteristics but even most importantly find their own voice and charisma and develop a public persona that embodies the brand they represent. A savvy public relations counselor will provide the resources and opportunities necessary, in some ways carve a path, for this person to become industry ambassador, diplomat to the Internet business community. In the following chapter, we look at some of the ways smart CEOs have fought back in the war on corporate image sabotage.

DAMAGE CONTROL: MANAGING ONLINE IMAGE

Now that we've heard about the new players in this game of digital public relations, we can explore what happens when these relationships turn sour, or why crises happen to good people. Despite all the planning, the preparation, the hard work, even foresight, crises happen. They are inevitable.

No matter how well thought out the plan, things can go wrong. It's part of the nature of human events. And to be sure, bad stuff will inevitably appear on the Internet about your company.

The idea is to make sure that bad things do not turn into a crisis. If you do not get to the source, information online can spread like wildfire. It's a cancer. If allowed to grow, once it reaches the print world, crises are typically out of control and the damage is almost overwhelming. The best thing to do is to confine it to the Internet, and, hopefully, to limited audiences on the Internet.

Fortunately, the Internet affords a measure of damage control that did not exist before. Now, instead of relying on others to filter the message, a one-to-one correspondence with the users and the media can occur, faster than almost any other mass medium affords

But the reverse is also true. In today's world, people without direct access to proper information or people who simply want to spread a bad rumor will run with something, and then there is a crisis that needs to be controlled.

Damage-control plans are particularly necessary in any new technology venture, as there are so many more opportunities for a company to make mistakes and/or deliver the wrong message about their plans that most companies certainly wind up developing such plans. Notwithstanding the bugs that inevitably plague any new process, there are issues of privacy, security, marketing, and child protection that can occur without warning on the Internet. Thus, vigilance is the eternal price for the freedom the Internet affords.

The cornerstone to online image control is being able to carefully monitor what is being said online about a company, a product, or even a corporate executive. When evaluating a business's preparedness to manage its online image, there are several questions to ask. Does the company regularly monitor Internet web sites and message boards? Does it have a program to determine what is to be considered significant information and what isn't? Does it have a process in place for dealing with those kinds of issues online after the determination is made that it is a serious problem? Who will deal with inaccurate information and how?

Presently, about 15 percent of the *Fortune 1000* companies have a good crisis communications program in place. And even of that tiny percentage of companies that may monitor the Internet to some degree, many do not have a full-fledged online crisis program, one that knows how to deal with an online image issue, online or offline. Table 8-1 presents some industries that have been behind as well as ahead of the curve in online crisis planning.

Some Internet companies, particularly those that have battled online rumors, have developed very sophisticated monitoring, analysis, and online communications programs. Those who have dealt with the existence of a rogue web site, a site offering unofficial, inaccurate, negative, and/or confidential information about a business, know too well the importance of these programs. Others are still pretty much in the dark ages.

There are still far too many companies that don't have an online reputation-management strategy. For far too many com-

Table 8-1   Industries with Good/Bad Online Image Management

GOOD	BAD
Technology	Energy
Airlines (some of the best, some of the worst)	Travel (general)
Consumer goods (where safety is concerned)	Consumer electronics
Advocacy groups	Insurance
Military	Telecommunications
Celebrities/musicians/entertainers	Banks
	Entertainment networks (cable TV, movie studios)
	Auto manufacturers
	Pharmaceutical companies

panies, the only online communications strategy has been to build a web site or online press-release archive and fast.

Often, that attitude leads to the misuse of the Internet, ignoring its bigger potential. Corporate executives often treat the Internet as a print medium, rather than an interactive component of an ongoing communications program.

That approach recalls a saying used in the old days of public relations. There are three things in the world that most clients want: they want things cheap, they want things fast, and they want things good.

The reality is that only two out of those three is usually achievable because things that are fast and cheap don't usually turn out to be great products.

That same formula holds true for the Internet. If an online image-management strategy is developed and implemented in a rush and lacks funding, it's not going to be good.

The watershed event for online crisis prevention and management goes back to Intel. By not reacting to an online warning from one of its users, the company spent billions of dollars in a product recall and received a battering to their image.

Intel, in some ways, deserved the negative attention at the time because it was not prepared to adequately respond to an Internet-born crisis.

In 1994, a professor in Virginia discovered a flaw in the first release of the much awaited Pentium chip. When doing complicated calculations, he discovered that this flaw made the calculations incorrect.

This, of course, was a very serious problem that could have affected lives in certain areas such as the space program, medicine, and public safety.

The professor tried to contact Intel about the problem, but did not obtain a satisfactory response. The company treated his complaint as something akin to a crank call.

However, this crank caller was not going away with a battle. The professor knew that the problem was too crucial to be ignored, so he turned to the public-spirited citizen's best complaint forum, the Internet.

He aired the flaw online in a Usenet newsgroup, and news of it soon spread like wildfire around the Internet. The message: Intel released a chip that had a flaw in it. Notwithstanding that it was a very minor flaw that was only going to cause errors in calculations in a small percentage of cases, consumers panicked.

Soon, *The New York Times* picked up what was going on and made it a major article in the Saturday business section.

Of course, at that point, the problem threatened Intel's business in a major way. After all, if its chips couldn't be relied on for calculations, then why would people buy computers built with them? It became a cause célèbre.

Instead of a minor problem, Intel then had a major crisis on its hands. It had to take back the product from anyone who had a chip, whether it was defective or not. Consumers were allowed to send it back to the company at Intel's expense and have it replaced.

Intel CEO Andy Grove, in his aptly named book, *Only the Paranoid Survive*, said that not following up with the professor and treating his complaint seriously was the single biggest mistake he ever made in business. It cost Intel half a billion dollars, and all because they did not respond to a simple e-mail.

There are many other cases of inappropriate management of online rumors and misinformation, and a continually growing number of sites that specialize in the posting of company mistakes, consumer opinion, hate postings, release of confidential information, and anticorporate activism.

Another landmark cybercrisis was faced by automotive giant Ford Motor Company with the site Flamingford.com. Again, a simple case of indifference to consumer complaints wound up costing the corporation millions of dollars. (See Figure 8-1.)

The Goldgehns, a couple living in Marietta, Georgia, had their Ford Ranger catch fire in the driveway in the middle of the night.

In the past, unhappy or mistreated consumers might call the company or the Better Business Bureau. In truth, there was very little they could do.

But in the Internet age, consumers have learned to strike back through the world's largest complaint forum. When Ford refused to acknowledge that the self-ignition of their new Ford truck was due to a manufacturing flaw, the Marietta couple put up a web site called Flamingford.com.

On some of the original home pages, the couple featured a picture of their car sitting in the driveway, burned to a crisp. They also explained their problem and encouraged other consumers with similar problems to get in touch.

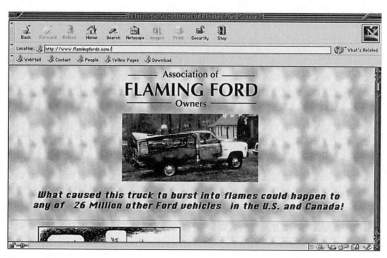

Figure 8-1

Then they started mounting a campaign strictly through e-mail, a grassroots effort that quickly built momentum and eventually caught the attention of the media.

You can guess the end result. Ford had to recall all of its allegedly fire-prone Ford Ranger trucks. *The New York Times* reported that the pressure put on by the Goldgehns was the single biggest reason for the recall, and estimated it cost Ford between $200 and $300 million, not to mention the cost of negative publicity.

Intel and Ford demonstrate important precedents for customer empowerment by the Internet. But there are other consequences for corporations that don't pay close attention to this thriving new medium.

In 1995 and 1996, corporate sabotage by disgruntled employees, competitors, and customers became something of a fad on the Internet. Several companies were harassed or had crucial materials, such as salary information, stolen and uploaded to bulletin boards.

Worse, in many cases, companies weren't aware that these messages were being spread. It was early in the history of the commercial Internet, and many simply weren't paying attention.

Up until early 1999, many CEOs were absolutely shocked about what they were seeing when shown message board postings taken from the Internet.

They simply had no idea what was out there because corporate communicators never visited these sites. The Internet was simply not a significant part of the company's communications program.

Several companies sheepishly admitted not heeding online discussions and chat postings until reporters began calling corporate spokespeople, seeking comment on a rumor or posting uncovered online.

One major movie representative watched painfully one night as a highly regarded television entertainment news show reported an online rumor about a troubled movie shoot that had been "uncovered" on a popular online movie chat group.

The executive later reported he felt like he had been blinded by the headlights of an onrushing vehicle. The rumor, of course, was not true, but it was being reported as gossip by a somewhat credible news outlet, thereby giving wings to its exposure.

In another significant case, a computer laptop manufacturer, EPS Technologies, only uncovered negative online discussion about its poor customer service when their CEO realized that sales numbers were drooping without any rational economic reason. After eliminating all logical explanations, the CEO arrived at the one he overlooked: the Internet. The problem was quickly addressed, but not without an impact to the company's financial picture and, notably, the company is out of business today.

Today, most traditional and emerging Internet-savvy companies understand that incorporating Internet discussion, news, and postings is a critical part of their communications function. Unfortunately, for some unlucky companies, that's mainly because they have read enough about the horror stories and seen the damage that can occur when there is no online ear to the ground.

For many years, the Recording Industry Association of America (RIAA) did not monitor the Pho list. They recently reconsidered. Despite a negative attitude about the site and a general dislike of digital downloads, it was important for the organization to accept the concept that this community was not going away, their opinions were influential, and then to understand it and communicate with it.

The problem was that organizations like the RIAA tend to respond emotionally when they see things that are inaccurate or damaging or somehow slanderous on a message board. Whether it's on some stock message board or a listserv mailing list, the gut instinct is to respond with emotion. It's understandable and human. It's also the wrong business move.

The biggest challenge for public relations professionals is to deal with these types of attacks on clients. Frankly, most of it is baloney, the sort of cocktail chatter that's long on rumor and short on information. A lot of it—perhaps 90 percent—should be ignored. But what about the 10 percent that is significant? If it isn't dealt with, and the chatter, rumormongering, and pseudo "news" builds momentum, it can cause major problems.

Remember: Bad news travels faster than good news. On the Internet, "news" often builds out from one newsgroup to five, and then the entire Internet, in the process getting further distorted and spiraling out of control. The public relations professional's job is to identify what information is potentially damaging and deal with it appropriately.

In the latest Middleberg/Ross study, better than half of all journalists admitted they will report on an online rumor if corroborated by a single source. That's one of the killers of a speedy world. It's no longer a multiple-source corroboration. Single-source corroboration is all it takes to print an online rumor.

Media competition is the reason. With so many news outlets dying to be No. 1, it's inevitable that delivering the news descends into a rugby scrum rather than a reasoned, careful approach.

Today, the media business is about thin staffs with an urgency to get news out before the next person. That allows, in some cases, for weak or shoddy reporting techniques, leading to companies getting into trouble.

The Internet can also be a source of corporate sabotage, where disgruntled employees, competitors, and angry customers all have an unfettered forum to air their complaints, much of it appearing to have the ring of truth to many non-discerning netizens.

Disgruntled employees can be the single biggest cause of problems online for a very simple reason: they have access to secret files and can make those documents suddenly appear online.

Even if they don't have the documents, disgruntled employees know what buttons to push. There are sites that specialize in this sort of water-cooler carping (Vault.com is a particular example) where all sorts of gripes about a parent company can be made by pseudononymous posters.

Of course, there are ample numbers of cases of employees harassing their companies that were documented years before the Internet became a mass medium. But the damage spreads so much faster on the Internet, calling for public relations professionals to heighten their vigilance about online comments.

Postings that receive significant traffic and distribution—for example, those on America Online and Yahoo! message boards—are essential for the public relations professional to monitor. Other must-reads include eComplaints.com and BoycottNews.com, which archive and present consumer and employee gripes about companies in a professional, credible manner and update consumers and activists on corporate boycotts, respectively. Not surprisingly, the airlines regularly top the list of complaint receivers online. (See Figure 8-2.)

Some of these chat rooms and web sites are more important and get more attention than others, but all have the potential to ignite controversy and cause damage to a client. Finding which chat rooms to monitor is more of an art than a science, but it takes good Internet instincts and a fair amount of experience with chat rooms to know where to look.

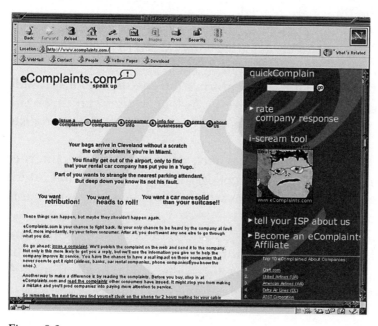

Figure 8-2

So Internet image researchers—i.e., public relations professionals—have to know which chat groups are peculiar to their clients and could possibly have the most influence, how to lurk in those chat groups, and how to make determinations about what's significant.

What today's companies literally need in place to gather the best online intelligence is a combination of eyeballs viewing chat rooms, excellent robotic searches that will hunt for key words or phrases automatically, and customized filters that will sift through hundreds of postings related to a company or specific incident.

Again, time is essential, and employee effort may not be as efficient as the electronic aides.

But the absolute minimum a firm can do is to monitor the Internet. A communications team has got be paying attention to what's being said about its organization online and be prepared to respond or they should be losing sleep at night.

Besides actual web sites, the Internet savvy public relations professional should also be a member of various e-mail lists (known as listservs) and Internet newsgroups, where postings on specific topics are placed.

There are also what's known as rogue web sites, i.e., sites that pop up that are deliberately constructed to hurt a company, product, service, or an individual.

Most of these sites have information that is libelous, totally false, and/or out of date. However, as long as they stay up on the web, they become major traps for potentially unwary journalists and/or rumor mongers.

It need not be a technical geek who monitors the Internet for a company. It could be a college intern, provided that intern receives the correct criteria by which he or she is going to report back the information.

Rather than trust an inexperienced intern's judgment, compile a checklist for the monitor that asks such crucial questions as whether the rumor could reduce sales, impact calls from 800 numbers, generate additional complaints, cause stock prices to fall, or lower employee morale.

In the end, online problems all add up to the same thing: they are damaging the client company. Now the public relations team has to deal with it.

One way to combat online rumor is to provide an updated, easy-to-use online media room for journalists and others to consistently obtain accurate information about your company. With all the information and misinformation available on the Internet, there needs to be a definitive source that a company can control and that has the correct information. If your company's web site is not that source, something is wrong.

Now, understand that providing information on your company isn't the same as controlling public perception of your company. Information is going to circulate on the Internet, and it's going to reach various information sources, some of them decidedly unfriendly to a company's objectives.

That's why it is so important to address the issues in the one forum you can control—your own site.

Many companies balk at the idea of putting anything but the most bland, upbeat messages on their own sites. They fear that by repeating the rumor, they will help spread the rumor. That is a very false concept. Giving correct information helps a company.

If something is true, it will be out on the Internet. If something is false, it will be out on the Internet. The key is to respond to that information, rather than to ignore it. Need we point out the public relations disaster that resulted from Exxon's infamous lack of response to the oil tanker *Valdez* crashing on an ecologically sensitive shoreline in Alaska?

It was 6 days before the company president first spoke on the subject. That was in 1989, way before the Internet was in most homes. Today, such a lack of response would be disastrous.

Other methods include becoming more familiar with the ways your online audiences interact with each other. It may seem obvious, but there is a proper and an improper way for a public relations person to visit a chat room.

The proper way is to simply watch the conversation.

The improper way would be to post messages that are unasked for or heavily commercial. That could cause more damage than the incident you're there to monitor.

Some chat rooms depend on what's known as a systems operator, or SYSOP, the equivalent of an online editor. In some cases, a web poster may need to run his or her credentials by this person for admission to a particular forum.

A corporate or public relations agency should never, ever hide its true identity on the Internet. Any attempt at deception will always bounce back to hurt the company's image, and could exacerbate any problems that already exist.

If something is false and posted on a newsgroup site, it can be handled in several ways, but, again, the key is speed.

The first step is to ask the SYSOP for help. Point out to the SYSOP that someone has posted an incorrect, damaging, and/or misleading statement. Most of the time, the SYSOP will want the correct information posted, and will allow a response to be posted.

If no SYSOP is involved, politely, but correctly, point out via a posted message that a previous message was incorrect.

Of course, public relations professionals could literally devote their entire existence to monitoring the Internet. There are that many postings on that many sites.

Clearly, a need exists for a trained evaluation of the material that comes in. For example, a message posted on a prominent Yahoo! or America Online board carries much more weight than something on an obscure Usenet board. It's far more likely to be seen by a greater number of people.

That's not to diminish the potential threat of the Usenet post. It's merely to point out the odds.

Not every negative post poses a credible threat. A post that rambles and makes all sorts of wild allegations will usually be seen as a rant by the Internet community in all but the most absurd circumstances.

But a trained public relations professional can usually spot the troubling posts. These are the ones that have a certain, authoritative tone, and are well written. They may, or may not, allude to print coverage or broadcasts in a vague, unspecified

Table 8-2   Identifying Volatile Information Online

Checklist of Important Information to be Handled Immediately if Found
Threats against company employees at any level.
Threats about consumer safety from any source.
Confidential or inaccurate information posted by company employees.
Negative or inaccurate information posted on a heavily trafficked, well-respected topical message boards such as Vault.com or iVillage.
Rumors or hearsay that are located in more than one chat group, web site, or discussion group and appear to be gaining acceptance.

way. These posts seek to generate momentum for bad information, and should be viewed as a serious threat. (See Table 8-2.)

Do employees react to news postings? Yes, they do. They read the medium as much as any other group, perhaps even more closely than some, given their stake in the company's well-being.

Some may feel the need to respond to posts that contain incorrect or potentially damaging information. While well intentioned, such "outside" public relations work should be discouraged. It's important for a company to speak with one voice, something that is increasingly difficult amid the cacophony of the Internet. (See Table 8-3.)

Numerous services have sprung up to help companies monitor online discussion, messages, web sites, and online publications.

Companies, like PRNewswire's eWatch, Net Currents, Web Clipping, and CyberAlert provide varying levels of virtual clipping services to alert clients to negative discussion and commentary that can avert potential communications disasters.

At the very least, these services help organizations take the temperature of public opinion, for better or worse.

Some companies have these services provide monitoring for their companies every day. It's usually too time-intensive an operation for small in-house public relations groups to do in an effective manner on a daily basis.

Table 8-3 HOW TO HANDLE MISINFORMATION

Do's

Do notify group users and webmasters or editors of inaccuracy.

Do notify key business partners, employees, and media of widespread inaccuracies.

Do respond on the company web site if the problem has reached a number of stakeholders.

Do understand that most companies and organizations have had to face online image issues. You are not alone.

Do treat stakeholder opinion online seriously. If someone has taken the time to post a comment or set up a web site, he or she is looking for some kind of response that they have not yet received.

DON'TS

Don't overreact.

Don't unleash the lawyers without a heavy dose of communications outreach. Don't expect a legal victory online to resolve an online image problem.

Don't expect the situation to go away overnight.

Don't ignore an online rumor or inaccuracy just because it's online and "no one will believe it."

Don't try to hide or cover up an online image problem that is indicative of a larger offline issue. The Internet community will quickly see through a lame public relations initiative.

In some cases, companies will hire a public relations firm to go in and take a snapshot for a period of 3 to 4 weeks. During that time, firms will look at almost every newsgroup and webzine and subculture form of communications on the Internet that will impact the company.

At the end of that period, the firm reports back to the company what they've found, provides a strategic program to deal with any issues that require attention, and recommends specific strategies and tactics.

We've talked about reactive strategies for using the Internet. Now let's examine some proactive ways that the medium can be used.

Most public relations specialists are conditioned to eternally be in a reactive mode. The problem with that strategy is that reacting often takes time, and in a world that moves at Internet speed, there often isn't the time to carefully plan and construct damage-control plans.

The key is to anticipate change or problems before they occur in order to stay on top of the matter. It's much better to have them already in place and ready to roll. In addition, a company that has developed a strong rapport with its online audience will have a much easier time helping that community receive and understand up-to-date, accurate information about their organization.

Great brands have strong online followings. These evangelists can be integral to a company's success online. BMG's music sites, Bugjuice.com, an alternative rock site, and Twangthis.com, a country music site, have built tremendous online followings through fan participation events and contests, and provide music fans with exclusive interviews and promotional material. These online fans are quick to "spread the word" on other fan sites and provide BMG with an ear to the street to see how their artists are faring. BMG is one company that has leveraged these online communities as an integral part of their overall communications program.

Another pharmaceutical company that manufactures products for infants and seniors was not as smart online. They recruited a group of moms who were paid to post promotional information about the company's products while they surfed online. The lack of authenticity with this strategy was transparent and ultimately, the online community flamed these moms out of business and left the pharmaceutical company embarrassed and with an online credibility problem on its hands.

The online communications efforts of an online trading property are not as black and white. The broker did a great job of promoting new services and features offline among its key online communities with discount offers and giveaways. The initiatives helped boost awareness offline and online and drove site traffic momentum. However, the company hadn't developed a rapport with its audiences online via email. Therefore, when a technical glitch occurred, the broker was unable to use the e-mail addresses of its customers because it could have sparked an inappropriate amount of fear and concern for customers who were unaccustomed to hearing from their online broker via e-mail.

Another tricky challenge is determining when something is a legal issue and when is it a public relations issue. The line is blurred, and erring on either side can be a problem.

Ultimately, every online image issue is a public relations issue. Legal action can often seem like corporate heavy handedness.

Let that perception leach out onto the Internet and you may have a problem bigger than the one you're trying to squelch. Look no further than the record industry's early attempts at curbing piracy. The very acts intended to combat the problem may have caused further problems by fanning the flames on the Internet.

Another example is Ford, which had an issue in 1999 with a web site that produced confidential information about Ford's new product line. Ford sued, but its legal initiatives were thwarted and the courts ruled the site could stay up as long as confidential corporate information was taken off the site.

The result was some serious backlash toward Ford's anti-Internet initiatives from the media, investors, and consumers. They thought it was very much overkill, kind of "Ford squashing the little guy." The resulting negative publicity attached to Ford was probably worse than the information revealed by the site.

Sometimes, however, legal action is inevitable. A company's interests can be seriously threatened, and third parties, such as corporate attorneys, compliance officers, human resources directors, and even the Securities and Exchange Commission, may have to be brought in to back up a company.

In all cases, the company's position should be laid out logically for the news media and consensus built before the announcements of such actions occur. Otherwise, the company again runs the risk of calling in the big dogs when a small poodle was all that was needed.

Despite best efforts by public relations professionals and their teams, it seems that every new development in combating misinformation online is countered by a new opportunity for corporate sabotage.

There are now investigative services that can be brought in to locate malicious web posters. However, new privacy policies are being implemented almost daily to protect the identity of online posters.

The main concern of most companies continues to be that when the media, potential customers, and potential employees look up a company's name for research in the search engines, anticorporate sites and posting links pop up.

Rogue webmasters are clever. They understand how to work the search engines, and know how to work the metatags, or key words that allow these sites to come up early in the search listing. If consumers see these rogue sites, they can be easily scared away from doing business with a company or dealing with a particular individual.

Whether or not a posting can be removed, if a bad message is out there, it's the public relations team's responsibility to make some determinations. The biggest is whether to bring that bad message to the public's attention on the company's web site.

Yes, it's a risk that some people will end up being informed of a problem they wouldn't otherwise have known about, but it's a proactive response that provides an opportunity to shape the message, rather than respond to someone else's message.

How the firm responds is another factor. Smart companies use their own web sites to at least present their points of view and establish links from their sites to other pieces of reference information that supports these points of view.

In one particular example of proactive rumor squelching, the U.S. Postal Service posted a statement on its web site refuting an online rumor that the organization supported a measure being pushed through Congress by a particular senator.

If a company doesn't want to address a touchy issue on its main site, some consider setting up a separate site just to deal with that one issue.

For example, a large consumer goods company was forced to combat a rogue web site established by an individual disputing copyright issues over the company's logo.

The company in question chose to contain the issue on the Internet by establishing a web site that gave all the facts about the history of the corporate logo, complete with legal documents and federal decisions in favor of the company.

The company also developed some pages to use in case the individual escalated her online campaign to other areas of corporate sabotage. In fact, the individual had threatened to launch a campaign linking the company's products to carcinogenic ingredients—a complete farce, but one that could have been exceedingly damaging and expensive to control and correct.

The last resort, if the problem is really serious, is to notify the media. If reporters are beginning to place calls, it's already too late to do anything but react.

It's also a good idea to have an idea how to respond when someone cold-calls and says, "We've just seen this online. How do you respond?" Communications executives must have a response to such queries prepared in advance or run the risk of fueling a larger crisis by responding inappropriately.

Of course, if those calls start escalating, public relations specialists must create and implement a larger targeted information distribution plan to address the online information issue.

Sometimes, crises are not Internet crises at all, but merely a failure to acknowledge the changing nature of communications.

Procter & Gamble had an issue in the spring 2000 when their stock dropped by approximately one-third in a single day. The drop was caused by a communications crisis. The company mishandled weak results for their first quarter.

A week before that drop, P&G executives were at a major industry conference exuding confidence. Instead of quietly preparing reporters and analysts, the company somewhat foolishly took an "all is well" position.

Thus, P&G caught the media and analysts totally by surprise when it made its announcement that profits would miss projections. Investors hate surprises. If you're an institutional investor, you've got large blocks of stock invested and a reputation to protect. Many analysts may have put an extra bitter spin on the P&G situation as revenge for the surprise.

Again, it was not an Internet crisis. But certainly one that could have been handled by some deft company spin on its own web site.

Absolute truth, defined as policies of honesty, candid communications, and frank online discussion, is the most important criteria for developing and managing a successful online image.

It is tremendously difficult, if not impossible, to try and finesse a bad situation online. The instant nature of communications leaves little wiggle room, and allows a quick response by a company's enemies.

Honest communications means constant communications. It means distributing information to as many audiences as possible, not to a select group of institutions, and developing interactive relationships with the online community that supports and embraces feedback, responsiveness, and two-way interaction.

At some point, if an organization has not established this level of online credibility, it will come back to haunt them. The role the Internet can play in damaging, building, and enhancing a company's reputation is no clearer than when looking at the Internet as a crisis communications tool.

THE INTERNET AS THE ESSENTIAL CRISIS COMMUNICATIONS TOOL

A *crisis*, by definition, is any situation that may threaten the integrity or perception of an organization and its leaders. It's a situation that is usually exacerbated by media attention.

In the event of a crisis, it's imperative that everyone—including consumers, investors, the media, and employees—obtain accurate information promptly from authorized corporate sources.

To achieve that, a company needs to have a comprehensive crisis communications plan in place before disaster strikes. And that starts with devising an online strategy because it's the fastest way to reach the most crucial people in a crisis.

The Internet has quickly become an essential component to a well-executed crisis management program.

Journalists, customers, and victims' families often look to the Internet as the first source of information about a company in crisis. That expectation can benefit companies if they incorporate the Internet into their crisis planning. It can also increase the frustration level for that same group of people if they find no information on the Internet.

The most notable examples of how crisis communications has been affected by this changing climate can be traced to two airline disasters.

In the first case, TWA's response to the explosion of its Flight 800 to Paris over the Long Island Sound was absolutely inadequate. The company stonewalled the media, in effect throwing gasoline on its predicament by failing to realize that the media was its conduit to the bereaved families across the United States.

Because TWA had no crisis plan in place, they looked uncaring, particularly in light of the sympathy expressed online by such diverse groups as the U.S. Navy, Boeing Airlines, and millions of grieving citizens around the world.

In fact, when one visited the TWA web site, there was no mention of the incident whatsoever, not even a press release or statement. By failing to update its site, the airline appeared uncaring not just to the online community but also to all the victims, and they were absolutely reamed in the press. That translates to a company's image, and certainly had an impact on consumer confidence in TWA in the months following the accident.

The lesson was duly noted by airline colleagues. When a major Swissair flight went down off Nova Scotia, that company handled Internet communications in a totally different manner.

Rather than ignore the ability of the Internet to instantly and globally communicate accurate, up-to-date information regarding the crash—and indicate the company's heartfelt sympathy for its victims—Swissair relied on the Internet as one of its most important crisis communications tools.

The Swissair team had tons of information posted in the hours following the crash, which largely helped to diffuse a terrible situation. The site was updated at least every 4 hours and was visited by reporters, family, concerned web users, and federal and nongovernment organizations.

In most situations, the public will understand if there is no new information and that it takes time to gather that information. But the public also wants to be assured they know what the company knows and that there is a conduit to the company that will respond to inquiries immediately.

By responding online, Swissair appeared on top of the situation, doing everything it could to facilitate communication.

* * *

One of the emerging tools of public relations wrought by the Internet is the proactive response to real-world disasters. A number of companies are prepared today to instantly erect a site, or portion of a site, that will deal with crises that erupt.

We've reached a point in the nature of the Internet as a mass communications medium where an instantaneous, global response to important news is an absolute necessity. So much so that an online financial information site was quoted in *The New York Times* as having "no comment" when the reporter discovered this company had no statement about a piece of breaking news on its web site.

The news cycle is now immediate, and no media will wait for a CEO to organize a press conference to report the facts. If the CEO is not available, rumor and speculation becomes the primary source of most news reports.

The issue could spin out of control by that point, and the company could look callous by its lack of response to an issue. It's almost a given that journalists, in times of crisis, will go to a company's web site for information.

Families will do the same. To not have the information they need posted online—and posted quickly—is communications incompetence.

In fact, companies who have not posted updated information on their web sites during a breaking news event have been cited as having "no comment" in publications as respected as *The New York Times*.

Companies run this sort of disaster control in different ways. Because crises and timing vary , there is no textbook way to do this.

A key part of that battle plan is a centralized communications point person, someone who can be contacted and get into action at a moment's notice. It does a company no good to spend precious hours to get its own act together. (See Table 9-1.)

Smart companies have made a contingency web site part of a strong crisis web strategy. These sites can contain updated official news statements, images and graphics, links to other

Table 9-1   Is Your Company Prepared to Handle a Crisis Online?

Does your crisis plan include online communications in addition to print and broadcast?

Does your crisis plan address Internet-born crises such as outage and security breaches?

Does your communications team have access to the corporate web site to deliver and distribute information via an online media room or contingency site?

Do you have at least one person designated to manage online communications in the event of a crisis?

Would your technology infrastructure support a double, if not triplefold, increase in site traffic within 12 to 24 hours?

Do you have relationships with online news sites and distribution channels to get news out quickly and globally?

Do you have an Intranet/Extranet communications plan to distribute news and updates to employees and business partners?

Can your company address cultural and linguistic logistics of communicating globally?

relevant sites, interactive features to communicate with the organization and/or connect with other online users, and a copious amount of background information relevant to the situation.

The goal is to make this online location an oasis of information that all important company audiences can use. It has to be considered the most helpful resource, or audiences will turn to less controllable sources of information, most with agendas that may exacerbate an already bad situation.

A perfect example is a contingency site created in case of a plane crash. The site should have the flight information ready to be filled in, the contact numbers in case of disaster, and some assurances that the company is working quickly to obtain information and do whatever is necessary.

At moments like that, assurances that something, anything is being done are of enormous comfort to those affected by the disaster, and give news organizations the impression that the company is in command. Such a perception will be translated and repeated in media reports, a crucial aspect of disaster control.

Such sites should be able to be launched at any time of day or night, usually by a chain of command that includes several executives reachable at a moment's notice. Any delay in response is potentially harmful to a company's interest. Thus, the contacts and authority to launch a disaster site must be in place well before it's needed. See Table 9-2 for a basic checklist to evaluate a company's preparedness to effectively handle a crisis online.

It's interesting that companies haven't had these sorts of chains of command in place for a long time. But it's even more amazing in the Internet age. Most major companies are well prepared if there was a *60 Minutes* expose, an article in *The New York Times*, or something in *The Washington Post*. They know exactly what to do and how to respond to those hypothetical situations. But the vast majority does not react and are not prepared to deal with a significant crisis via online communications.

Particularly savvy organizations are even taking proactive steps online to halt a crisis before it happens. Right before ABC's *20/20* planned to air a potentially damaging interview uncovering the

Table 9-2   Checklist for an Effective Contingency Web Site

☐   News releases

☐   Statements updated frequently during crisis peak

☐   Offline and online contact information

☐   Images and photos

☐   Maps, diagrams, and figures

☐   Background information on relevant people, products, and events

☐   Links to helpful resources

☐   Links to helpful news sites

☐   Searchable archive of information and past news releases

☐   Video and audio footage, if applicable

☐   Legal documentation

☐   Third-party testimonies and quotes

☐   Chronologies

☐   And extra bonuses:

    ☐   Ability to receive updates via email and pager

    ☐   Interactive informational guides

supposedly life-threatening dangers of diet pill Metabolife, the public relations response was for Metabolife to beat ABC to the punch. The company posted the uncut video of the interview with its chief executive on its site, reasoning that the best defense was an online offense. The ability to reach a mass audience before 20/20 had the chance to air the edited video allowed the company to seize control of the story. Metabolife wanted the public to know that it had nothing to hide, and wanted to eliminate the possibility of 20/20 editing and slanting the video to taint Metabolife's image. The public relations efforts behind the move also included a full-page ad in *The New York Times* directing traffic to the site. Metabolife reported over a million visitors downloaded the interview in the first 24 hours of its posting online. For Metabolife, this was a pure public relations victory. For ABC, it was a backhanded blow to one of its most popular, respected news shows.

Another example of using the Internet to reroute a potential crisis is with a popular Internet brokerage firm. On a Friday afternoon, the company was alerted to a scathing news story that was scheduled to run in the following Monday's print edition of *The New York Times*. The journalist had unearthed some negative background material on a partner who used to be associated with the company and intended to use this information to cast doubt on the company's current practices, which for all purposes were legitimate and without any hidden agendas. Recognizing the power of the Internet news media to spread information quickly to all corners of the globe, the company public relations counsel contacted a respected online news journalist on Friday afternoon and leaked the story revealing truths and nuances about the situation *The New York Times* reporter hadn't bothered to investigate. On Saturday and Sunday, the story spread online, a story that disconnected the former partner and his shady background completely from the ongoing business at the brokerage. By Monday, *The New York Times* story was old news and the potential crisis had been tamed and averted.

For every company that has failed to leverage the Internet to reach its audiences in times of crisis, there's another that has reached millions instantly. While TWA was criticized for its minimal online mention of its Flight 800 disaster in 1996, Alaska Airlines kept users up to date on its own flight disaster by posting a toll-free information number, as well as ongoing updated information on its site.

Media and communications experts have identified the key steps to preventing and managing a crisis online. From damaging online rumors in e-mail and Usenet groups, to "rogue" web sites and hack attacks, to offline corporate disasters which have migrated online, there are important steps companies can take in crisis communications. (See Table 9-3.)

One thing that damage control discussion points out is that the online world has forever changed the news cycle. The process of communicating to the media has changed in that as much of what the public sees on the 6 o'clock news is the result of what appears in the morning newspapers.

Now, much of what appears in the morning newspaper is a result of what appeared on web sites only hours earlier. Print journalists are reading their favorite web sites for story ideas, and those story ideas are then appearing in print and then migrate to broadcast.

It's not that one medium is more important than the other. As a mass medium, nothing has replaced television. But the rise

Table 9-3   Five "Must-Do" Steps in Using the Internet to Manage a Crisis Situation

* Take preventative measures: create a contingency web site or a strategy for possible crisis situations.

* Establish relationships with key online news sites (Associated Press, CNN, MSNBC) to ensure the most updated and accurate content is posted on their sites if a crisis occurs.

* Act online immediately.

* Be proactive in posting information, so the online community doesn't hear the news elsewhere. Companies such as MediaLink offer live webcasting of press conferences and related event.

* Make a commitment to be honest and consistent throughout the site, cater to both the media and the public, and offer as much information as possible, including toll-free phone numbers, updates, and an online press center.

of the Internet has augmented and influenced how TV covers breaking news.

For prestige, *The Wall Street Journal* and *The New York Times* are still the kings for business news. But if one looks at how a story appears, or how it grows, or how misinformation can go from one medium to the next, the source of all major news information, because of its timeliness, starts with the online world.

In fact, the whole process of a press conference has changed. Even during a crisis, corporate public relations specialists used to call a press conference at 10 o'clock in New York, and give journalists in other parts of the country press materials a few days in advance, with the clear understanding that the information was to be embargoed until a particular time.

The famous Johnson and Johnson Tylenol tampering scare took 8 days to be managed. Today, that time frame would be unthinkable.

Now, if a company calls for a press conference and provides information in advance, journalists are no longer able to hold to the embargo. The competition is so severe that the understanding now is if a journalist gets the information, it's going to go out. And where is it going to go? It's going to go on the web site. That makes the point of most press conferences moot.

This acceleration of information from place to place is so phenomenally advanced that one really has to think through the process of giving out information. Timing is everything, particularly with announcements that aren't hot news. Public relations professionals have to be sure that their clients give the news to a source that will, in turn, run with a story and therefore lessen the chances of other news organization coverage.

Take a publication like *Business Week* or *Fortune*, which publish every 2 weeks.

In the past, a public relations professional would meet with an editor from *Fortune* knowing they would have 6 to 8 weeks before a story would appear, thanks to the print publication schedule. That meant the public relations team could give out the information and know that the story would break according to the editorial calendar.

But now, if a corporate spokesperson meets with a *Fortune* or *Business Week* editor, that same editor also writes for the web site for that particular publication. The information goes out immediately.

Communications executives can no longer give out information without expecting it to become public immediately, and that changes a lot of the off-the-record comments that might be dispensed. It also changes a lot of the information that public relations specialists would use to curry favor with journalists by giving them advance scoops with more information. That practice is no longer appropriate today.

In contrast to the instantaneous news needs of crisis communications, trade shows and other face-to-face opportunities are still as important as they ever were in the news process.

Public relations, despite the advances and changes incurred in the hi-tech world, is still a hi-touch area. That will always take precedent over hi tech.

Personal relationships still make or break relationships between a company and its customers, a media organization and a publicist, and an agency and its clients.

Crisis communication plans that rely solely on the process of communications will not be as successful as those that consider relationships and people first. The art of having lunch with a journalist is becoming a forgotten art, and its importance is being undervalued. In times of crisis, a relationship built on trust, credibility, and partnership, forged over time, will be crucial to conveying the message that the company wants the public to hear. An anonymous voice on the phone carries less credibility than a familiar face. And it takes time to build those relationships.

During a crisis, companies need to exercise special attention to a multilingual communications campaign that addresses a global, diverse clientele.

Understandably, all translation options require time. For this reason, the company must publish all information in English as soon as it is complete and post additional translations as they become available. However, since crisis documents are typically short in length, foreign translation time is relatively negligible.

In fact, at the most critical moments of a crisis, a corporate statement is usually less than 80 words.

A company's language translation capabilities should address three communication issues inherent in global communications.

First, it must be sensitive to cultural nuances. It is not enough to provide mere literal translations of key information related to the crisis. The client will have to reinforce its image as an international brand by offering information relevant to all visitors, regardless of geographic or cultural idiosyncrasies. This will necessitate a language-translation capability that meets the needs of each major nationality.

Second, the language translation must be available as soon as possible. The time between final drafting and complete translation must be minimal in order to update all foreign site visitors continually.

And third, it must be constantly on call. As with all crisis resources, translation capability should be available at all times regardless of time or date.

To meet these conditions, a company must rely on human translators, in addition to computer software. Translation technologies provided by companies like eLingo, MicroStream, or AltaVista do not adequately translate important crisis documents. Additionally, language translation firms like Berlitz Translation Services provide on-call translation capabilities that address cultural nuances and are executed quickly.

The overall objective of an effective online crisis plan is to promptly provide information, communicate the corporate message, and alert outsiders that a corporate interest or organization will be diligent in keeping in touch and providing information when available.

In particular, the goals of a program should include demonstrating the client's concern for the safety of all parties (e.g., customers, employees, etc.), communicating promptly and honestly the client's position to all relevant audiences, voiding any negative media attention, and positioning the client in a positive light.

When evaluating whether to prepare a contingency web site to reach out to the global audience in times of significant crisis, smart businesses have identified situations that can be eased tremendously by use of a separate site.

1. *Mass casualties*: This includes incidents that occur due to the alleged negligence of the client. Examples include serious accidents, food poisoning, or death due to natural or unnatural causes. Although morbid to consider, pharmaceutical companies, food producers, and businesses in the travel industry are prone to crises of this nature.

2. *Natural disasters*: Significant damage/casualties caused by environmental-related incidents. These can include fire, severe weather, environmental toxins, fatal radiation, or earthquakes. Energy companies and governmental organizations are often asked to respond quickly during these situations, sometimes merely by their association with the crisis.

3. *Large-scale legal matters*: This can include a massive, long-term legal attack, such as that endured by Microsoft during its antitrust litigation. Because litigation can cover a broad spectrum of issues, including negligence, fraud, or criminal matters, a client may choose to establish a crisis plan for select issues. To qualify as a serious crisis, plaintiffs in this instance would have to be on the grandest scale. American Express and Nike are two household brands that have taken their legal issues to the Internet by providing updates, company statements, and updates in times of legal involvement.

Many of today's practices are based on the watershed example Bell Atlantic set back in 1996 when it established a web site specifically to address the Telecommunications Act of 1996. It quickly became the leading source of information for a disparate group of reporters.

While all outsiders will be monitoring a company's activities during a crisis, it is important to provide customized and relevant information to all key parties. Table 9-4 lists specific audiences and what they look to find on the Internet during crises.

Table 9-4 Who Looks for What During a Crisis?

Audience	Rationale	Needs
Media	Journalists are increasingly looking to the Internet during moments of crisis. In addition to traditional media sources (e.g., *The New York Times*, ABC news, local print and broad-cast outlets, etc.), this category also includes unofficial company sites that purport to disseminate client news.	Crisis updates Corporate position Contact information Corrective measures
Employees	During a crisis, communicating to employees should be as important as communicating to the press or customers. In addition to general news and information, employees will be looking to the Internet to find general guidance on how the crisis will affect their daily affairs. For example, if the crisis is directly related to employee life (e.g., a labor strike), labor unions will be closely monitoring the company's Internet presence.	Crisis updates Corporate position Media policy Contact information Emergency procedures
Victims and those impacted by the crisis	In addition to a corporate message, the company must provide a detailed and objective explanation of the crisis. While victims, or those associated with the impact of the crisis, will primarily be searching for news and information, the Internet allows the company to express corporate concern and condolences, if necessary. This differentiates "crisis response" from "corporate responsibility."	Crisis updates Corporate explanation Contact information Corrective measures Emotional and compensation counseling Grievance or complaint channels (chat, community, etc.)

Stakeholder	Description	Information needs
Customers	In order to proactively communicate past and future damage prevention measures, the company must explain all its emergency procedures on the Internet. This can include evacuation procedures, weather forecasts, and transportation issues. In addition, the company can use the Internet as a forum to publicly acknowledge any inconveniences and provide compensation options for all those affected.	Crisis updates Corporate explanation Contact information Compensation Emergency procedures
Evangelists and influencers	So-called evangelists, such as analysts and the media, will be looking to the Internet to understand the ramifications of the crisis and how it may affect any other company offerings.	Crisis updates Corporate explanation Counseling recommendations and tactics
Local community	The company must preserve its relationship with the community by explaining frankly how the crisis will affect the local area and business community.	Crisis updates Corporate position and explanation Compensation Corrective measures
Government and regulatory bureaus	During a crisis, it will be important to address organizations, both governmental and trade.	Compensation Crisis details Contact information
Legislators	The Internet provides an opportunity to demonstrate the company's dedication to solving the crisis. Legislators will look to the Internet as an extension of corporate communications activities and will be searching for any illegal or damaging claims.	Corporate position Corrective measures
Third-party advocates	Environmentalists, activists, and consumer advocates will be looking to the company to provide explanations of the crisis.	Crisis updates Corporate position and explanation Contact information

A company's objective should never be to pretend nothing is wrong or avoid the situation but to communicate accurate information protecting the corporate interest and reinforcing the company's brand.

Is your team ready for a disaster? Run down this checklist and see. Answering yes to all of these questions will indicate your company is equipped with the resources necessary to proactively communicate the client's messages and crisis-response policies online.

1. *Develop an online crisis team*: In order to delegate responsibilities and manage all communications in the event of a crisis, an online crisis team must be in place. It should be comprised of senior-level management, public relations executives, web site designers, and, if necessary, legal counsel. The objective of the team will be to ensure the prompt dissemination of news and information online.

2. *Online crisis team organization and structure*: An Online Crisis Communications Team should meet on a quarterly basis to review crisis protocol and train new team members. The team should study similar crises on an ongoing basis and discuss how the plan can be improved. For example, at many of the leading airlines, crisis communications teams have an ongoing internal discussion group on the company Intranet. The group confers about how any particular airline is handling a crisis. It is important to maintain a fluid and constant flow of information within the group to ensure preparedness for any major crisis.

3. *Create a crisis news site*: As the cornerstone of the online communications plan, the crisis news site is a microsite designed to centralize and control information flow in the event of a disaster. The site should be completely distinct from the consumer site and the media site. The crisis URL should be easily associated with the client and the crisis at hand, while existing independently of the main promotional sites.

   Suggested URLs for such a crisis site include the following generic examples: XYZCompanyUpdate.com, XYZcompanyHelpCenter, and XYZBulletin.com.

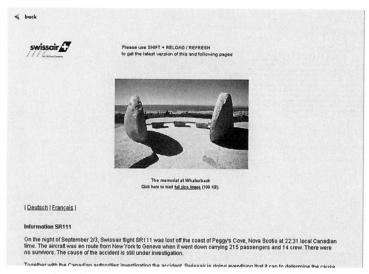

Figure 9-1

The purpose of the site is to provide immediate, accurate, and comprehensive information managed and edited by the client. Prepared in advance and kept inactive until the actual crisis, the crisis news site becomes the source for all relevant information online. For example, Swissair has garnered praise for its web site during the crash of flight SR111. (See Figure 9-1.)

The site was updated on an ongoing basis and included language translation, multimedia, contact information, and corporate statements. In addition, the tone and visual aspect of the entire site remained consistent with the public contrition of the company—plain white and minimal.

In addition, during the crisis, the URL should serve as a symbol of the company's corporate response. It can be used in offline advertising or mentioned by the company spokesperson during press conferences. This will refer inquiries to the client's official crisis news site and avoid any potential damage caused by media bias.

4. *Contents:* The crisis news site should be designed to maximize navigability and ease-of use Additionally, the site should be extremely thorough with exhaustive information related to the

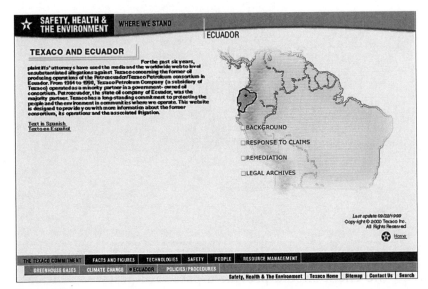

Figure 9-2

crisis. For example, Intel's pressroom is more than 10 layers deep, offering multimedia, biographies, speeches, philanthropy profiles, product details, and in-house contact information.

That site is a "best-practice" example of how to maximize the Internet and have journalists rely primarily on official corporate sources.

Another strong example is Texaco's use of the Internet to respond to allegations of improper operations in Ecuador. (See Figure 9-2.)

The site offers elaborate resources in Spanish and English, including background, response to claims, remediation, and legal archives. In particular, a site should adequately address the following four categories: home page, online media room, victim resource center, and corporate Intranet.

HOME PAGE—THE CRISIS PORTAL

On the first screen of the crisis news site, users should have access to all major site components related to the crisis. The actual page should be plainly designed and include direct access to:

- Updated news
- Corporate statement (letter from the chairperson)
- Emergency response
- Contact information
- Q&A

THE ONLINE MEDIA ROOM

For members of the press interested in learning more about the crisis, the client should provide a password-protected site that addresses all major media concerns, including multimedia, updates, and background information. Journalists should be allowed to subscribe to news in the form of registered news alerts in specific time increments (via e-mail paging, mobile communications, etc.).

In addition, members of the press should be given the opportunity to interact with the client's officials. This communication includes e-mail, online press conferences, and, potentially, chat rooms. Specifically, a "best of class" media room includes:

- Paging capabilities
- Multimedia (e.g., video, audio, and still photo)
- Access to online press conference, with video archives of past conferences
- Speech transcripts and other related documents
- Contact information

For example, Boeing has created a comprehensive newsroom that addresses up-to-the-minute developments as well as past crises that affected the company. (See Figure 9-3.)

It has been regarded as a "best practice" example that offers streaming video, corporate statements, and archived speeches.

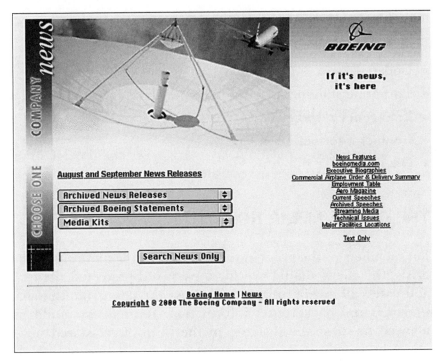

Figure 9-3

VICTIM RESOURCE CENTER

In the event of a massive disaster, resources available to victims and victims' families should allow for direct contact with the client's executives, counseling resources, and other victims (if appropriate).

The site must give the online community an opportunity to grieve and interact with the company and each other. In addition, the site should indicate that personal inquiries could be made via the toll-free crisis hotline.

For example, inquiries on specific casualty names should not be made online as the company is in danger of appearing to respond to specific crisis situations in a generic fashion. Specifically, the victim resource center should contain:

- Chat rooms
- User feedback

- Emotional counseling contacts
- The client contact information (e.g., management, crisis team, public relations, etc.)

CORPORATE INTRANET

The client and all other company employees should also have the opportunity to access relevant information online via the company Intranet. Even while off the grounds and away from work, employees should be able to access the corporate Intranet via passwords. Specifically, the site should offer:

- A media policy
- Evacuation procedures
- User feedback
- The client contact information (e.g., internal communications, managers, etc.)

ESTABLISH ONLINE TOOLS FOR PROACTIVE MEDIA OUTREACH

An integral part of the crisis communications plan will be a strategic campaign to reach the media in a proactive fashion. In addition to using the crisis site and aggregated news sources to disseminate information, it will be important to maximize Internet sources to provide diverse content and rich presentations. There are many Internet services that facilitate the dissemination of news during times of crises.

When appropriate, a company should use the Internet to send journalists any multimedia information related to the crisis. In particular, still photos, audio samples, and video footage can all be delivered to reporters via Internet-based services like Medialink and BusinessWire, or via e-mail as an attachment. These companies do not require a great deal of notice and could help develop a multimedia presentation efficiently.

It is important to ensure that a journalist is interested in receiving content before actually delivering it via e-mail. The 1999 Middleberg/Ross Print Media in Cyberspace Study indicates that while an increasing number of journalists look to the Internet for research, they are still hesitant to receive e-mail attachments without just cause.

In particular, the client should look to the Internet to create an online press conference. Companies like Medialink help broadcast live events across the Internet. The client can designate private audiences or the general press in announcing relevant news related to the crisis.

While DoubleClick's recent privacy bout is certainly not a good example of crisis management, the company made sure to link its archived privacy conference to its web site. Now, as journalists look for information, they are "met" by the company spokesperson, in this case, CEO Kevin O'Connor.

Companies should take special note of the individual services each of these news sites offer. Yahoo! (and others) offer pages dedicated to one individual and to ongoing stories. For example, Yahoo!'s section on the Microsoft antitrust trial contains updated news stories from various online newspapers and magazines, extensive news archives, audio and video news clips, related Internet sites detailing issues relevant to the trial (such as legal resources), message boards containing discussion of the trial, and links to other aspects of the Microsoft corporation. It should be considered inevitable that Yahoo! will erect a section of their site dedicated to a crisis at the client, and the company must make sure Yahoo! has the most updated, accurate, and diverse information possible.

Companies that have an enormous presence on the Internet should be aware that, in addition to the heavy online media coverage, an abundance of unofficial sites dedicated to brands exist. These sites carry a lot of influence when it comes to the online and offline perception of a company.

Fans often look to fan sites as often as they do commercial news sites or official fan sites for updated information. Fan sites also contain message boards and chat rooms, where users can comment about the information offered. In fact, webmasters of the most popular fan sites are often quoted as sources in stories.

Given the global nature of the company's brand and the international audiences that would be affected by a crisis at the client, it is crucial to offer information in relevant languages.

These languages should be determined based on park surveys and international queries. Most U.S. crisis sites include the more popular languages (e.g., English, Spanish, German, and French). Language translation is a "must have" and is an indication to the media of the company's concern to address all affected parties (similar to the client's international site).

The translated sites should not have separate URLs and should be clearly linked from the crisis news home page. Or, as Swissair demonstrates, one page can hold multiple language translations of the same content (Swissair.com).

A growing trend in crisis management is the use of customized responses to specific language, cultural, and geographic needs. It is not enough to offer standard American design and content translated into different languages.

Audiences will have different needs and design preferences specific to their interests and geography. Regardless of such circumstances, all visitors to the site should be able to interact with the content in the same comprehensive fashion, including chats and messaging.

The specific language sites should address geographic needs as well. For example, the site should provide travel information for a tourist from Japan who is concerned about travel arrangements. The site should offer specific links to airlines, travel agents, and weather information.

It is also a given that crisis sites will generate extremely high traffic. Thus, it is crucial to keep in mind the possibility of a hacking attempt. This could potentially cause a service stoppage, or even more severe, insert false information onto the site. In the event of a successful hacking attempt, the client should remove the site immediately.

The client should also have a statement written prior to the incident that explains the technical difficulties and contact information that can be referred to for accurate information (e.g., toll-free number, other links, etc.).

Many sites have experienced hacks during high-traffic crisis periods. ValuJet's web site, for example, was hacked shortly after its well-publicized Everglades crash in the fall of 1997. (See Figure 9-4.)

To protect the site from such attacks, it is necessary to have a number of backups of the site on various remote servers.

It is also important to work with site programmers to ensure that a sudden boost in site visitors will not jeopardize the efficacy of the site. Administrators should be prepared to place the crisis site on remote servers at any given notice and channel click-throughs efficiently.

For instance, Alaska Airline officials made the decision to move certain section of its web site, including the home page and the section devoted to Flight 261, to different web servers in order to handle the huge increase in volume.

When a crisis occurs, a company should augment its online monitoring programs, placing the emphasis on searching for

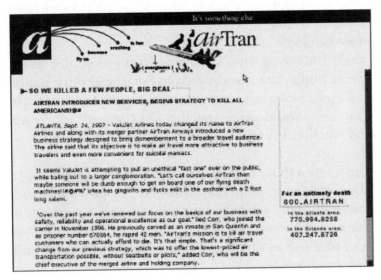

Figure 9-4

discussions related to the crisis at hand. It is crucial that monitoring be conducted at least daily—more often, if possible—and that a company pay particular attention to prevalent rumors that are inaccurate in any way.

The company need not respond to postings. Rather, it should use the Internet to remain aware of the sentiments and rumors circulating online in the event of any direct inquiries by the media or other interested parties.

To reinforce the company's condolences and appearance in the media, it will be important to withdraw all advertising and promotional materials that exist online. In the event of a serious crisis, the client will need to proactively contact all advertising partners and promotional outlets to ensure that the client adequately withdraws itself from consumer attention.

Industry experts claim that the effectiveness of a crisis management campaign is determined within the first 24 hours. Prompt response is critical to the success of a crisis program, and the client will have to capitalize on the immediate nature of the Internet to adequately respond to a crisis of massive scale.

It is also critical for the client to manage corporate communications, media, and public relations after the crisis even though the initial shock and trauma may have dissipated. This includes traffic monitoring, archiving information, and posting corrective measures.

As a measurement of the program's effectiveness and as a potential promotional tool, it is important to consistently monitor the traffic of the crisis news site. Ultimately, the quantification of crisis site traffic can be used as an indication of effective corporate response.

In addition, noticing what parts of the site are the most popular will help determine the need for any possible expansion or diminution of content.

The lack of appropriate site monitoring proved to be a major flaw in Alaska Air's handling of its crisis earlier this year. Its crisis site was so consumed with page views that officials decided to turn off the traffic counter and allow for faster page downloads. As a result, the airline has been unable to accurately communicate the effectiveness of its crisis response.

Another valuable technique for site traffic monitoring is to measure site movement by individual IP address. This will help determine the relationship between visitors and specific areas.

Of course, if this technique is used, it will be imperative to post all tracking practices on the site's privacy policy section.

After a crisis, many companies attempt to minimize its importance by neglecting to post archived corporate statements. This carelessness is a clear indication to outsiders that the company has not adequately acknowledged the crisis.

TWA, for example, has yet to post significant recognition of the Flight 800 tragedy. Companies like Boeing lead the way in contrition and corporate responsibility by outlining the corporate statements for all major airline crashes within the past few years.

In addition, archiving multimedia enhances a site's presentation and allows the client to editorialize its content appropriately.

In addition to archiving information related to communications, the client should use the site to demonstrate the steps being taken to make sure that such a will not happen again.

For example, Nike outlined its employee policies after allegations of abusive labor practices in the developing world. Another example is Swissair, which currently posts a picture of a monument built in memoriam of those that died in the flight.

Now that we've discussed reaction to a crisis, let's take a look at one of the more effective proactive tools created by the rise of the Internet: viral and online community marketing.

VIRAL PUBLICITY— BUILDING COMMUNITY AND AWARENESS ONLINE

Without a doubt, no area of public relations is growing faster than online communications. The Internet has brought forth a new communications dynamic that melds traditional public relations with online one-to-one marketing. The opportunities are tremendous—and so are the perils.

While the Internet allows for more targeted, informal outreach techniques, it also turns several bedrock assumptions of public relations on their heads.

First, the Internet is an environment of dialogue, not monologue. A disseminated article or press release can potentially elicit immediate response from the consumer audience, creating an open exchange of ideas. It can also elicit a massive wave of negative feedback if the placement of that release is inappropriate or its subject matter rubs people the wrong way.

Second, the Internet is both targeted and scattered. Consumers can be reached one to one, but the same message may also inadvertently reach journalists, competitors, investors, and others who need to hear a different message.

The negative potentials have been clearly outlined in a previous chapter—let's focus on the positive. The good news is the distance between business and consumer is rapidly closing. This should be seen as an enormous opportunity to get to know your customers better and empower them to drive your communications initiatives.

A handful of savvy firms now have a special division devoted to online publicity, and advanced companies have integrated these practices with their marketing and public relations departments. What they're doing is wholly different from the traditional public relations role of contacting journalists and placing stories.

While a lot of the same principles of offline marketing apply in the online world, online publicity allows you to reach individuals one to one, whereas, in the offline world, it's a one-to-many relationship. Obviously, the former allows more customized communication and the potential to develop a long-lasting exchange.

Businesses are implementing the technology to allow them to target their messages and match these with their audiences, and more and more marketing people now understand that online publicity is something they have to do. Often, public relations specialists have read a lot of press about search-engine optimization and e-mail marketing being extremely effective in creating new customers and sustaining relationships with the customers they already have, and they want to be on board with this program.

The problem for many of them is they just don't know how to do it. There's a lot to learn when undertaking an online versus an offline publicity campaign. Some of the same principles apply, but many of them are very different. There are many strategies unique to the Internet, where things like personalization, copy length, and what types of words entice people to open up an e-mail can be critical to the success or failure of a marketing campaign.

One of the best features of online publicity is the measurability. Next to search engines, e-mail is the second best way to reach a target audience. Click-through rates for an e-mail with a link back to a home page ranges from 5 to 22 percent.

When undertaking a campaign, it's best to strive to take it to an extremely personal, grassroots marketing level.

Online publicity is very niche-oriented. It's very viral, moving from person to person. If something is good, funny, sick, helpful, or silly, inevitably humans will want to share it with others. The Internet allows them to easily do that. Viral marketing is like a grassroots campaign, the equivalent of going door-to-door, neighbor to neighbor.

It's the one area where advertising agencies and public relations interactive agencies are beginning to understand how terrific the online community can be when trying to promote products and services to consumers. They've already seen the results.

New Line Cinema is one particular example of a company using the Internet in a wise way. New Line Cinema looks to the Internet to drive traffic to upcoming movie releases via viral marketing.

For example, to promote the movie, *Final Destination*, the company began its campaign with banner advertisements. When visitors went to the film's site (*www.deathiscoming.com*), they were able to forward postcards of minipromotions of the upcoming film to friends and family.

This viral campaign allowed tens of thousands of people to view the promotion trailer before the release of the movie.

Bertelsmann Music Group (BMG) is another example. BMG has a genre-specific music hub, Bugjuice, that's used to promote its artists and new releases. When it launched, it began to announce its arrival and offerings by placing targeted messages on message boards.

One of the first big promotions for the site was a webcast by recording artist Natalie Imbruglia. The online team for BMG would go out and find her fans on the Internet, tracing various message boards and homesteading sites, and let them know that there was an upcoming concert by their favorite artist.

Homesteading sites, or personal home pages, are particularly rich soil. GeoCites and Xoom fans have already proven their loyalty by going through the motions of constructing a site. Natalie Imbruglia fans were only too happy to become a part of the "team" by placing graphic links on their sites that would drive traffic to the webcast.

Traditional and online advertising of the show would not have been a great way to drive traffic. First, it's not very targeted, and second, the click-through rates on banners are abysmal, something on the order of .5 percent or lower.

It's much better to identify someone who's specifically interested in the topic. Yes, it's somewhat painstaking, but it's not about quantity. Finding five or ten message boards that are active will result in a pass-around rate to other fans, virally building exposure to a highly targeted audience.

The Natalie Imbrugila concert was highly successful. With just 1 week of promotion, Bugjuice managed to attract 4000 registered users.

Reaching the greatest number of people online is always a matter of looking in the right place. Frankly, chat groups are not a great way to market a company. The reason is that none of the chat is archived, so reaching that group of people becomes a scattershot approach. Maybe the key constituents who will help you spread the word are in the chat room at the time you visit. Most likely, they are not or may be, in fact, hostile to your attempts at viral marketing.

Truly effective online publicity and marketing is more about reaching a constituency through message boards. Message boards are archived and searchable. The message will be available on demand for all to see for a relatively long period in Internet time.

One thing to remember, however, when promoting on these boards is that you can't merely go up on a board and say, "buy my cell phone." You'll be flamed into eternity, if anyone cares to respond at all.

Public relations and viral marketing teams have to find people who are looking for specific content, and then provide them a service by directing them to the content they're seeking. Thus, it's not recommended to use message boards to promote e-commerce companies who do not have rich content that will be helpful to a potential user.

To be sure, companies can be proactive about building online relationships. One way to direct traffic is to introduce a message on a board akin to, "I happened to be looking at this site and found this great information on users for cell phones that some of you may not have heard about."

The stuff that's clogging the boards is people trying to promote their products and services in a blatant, in-your-face manner. Those are the boards that eventually close for lack of interest, overwhelmed by the weeds of advertising.

If you go to deja.com, you'll see the dismal results of such unfettered commercials. Hundreds of the same messages dot dead boards, screaming, "buy my products" to a ghost audience. It's hard to find message boards with quality content, but they're still out there. Those are typically ones with strong moderators, who root out the advertisements before they take root and kill the board.

Another key aspect to online viral marketing is called opt-in e-mail, or permission-based marketing. It involves asking someone for his or her permission to send more information later, with the understanding that what is sent will be of interest.

E-mail is usually the No. 1 reason people use the Internet. Surveys have found that somewhere near 80 percent of the Internet's population is likely to respond favorably to an opt-in e-mail. That's in contrast to the 30 percent of the population that indicates it's likely to respond favorably to non-opt-in, or SPAM, mail.

In short, this is one of the most successful of all the online marketing campaigns. The successes are sometimes incredible. For example, with Sesame Street, one of its direct e-mail programs achieved a 20 percent return. That's amazing when you consider that a traditional direct-mail campaign is considered a raging success with a 2 percent return rate.

How did a company like Sesame Street achieve such a great return? First, it has a very strong brand. Second, it had the right offer, a "Tickle Me Elmo" CD that was sold at a 50 percent discount. And third, it had a very targeted audience because it purchased the correct e-mail lists from a brokerage house that sells such names.

As they do with traditional direct mail, brokerages exist that will provide targeted addresses from customers who have purchased similar products or fit a very specific demographic. For instance, in the case of Sesame Street (see Figure 10-1), the

Figure 10-1

company wanted to reach parents, particularly women who had young children.

Such houses charge from 15 to 50 cents per e-mail address. Although those costs can add up, they're well worth it.

Once a mailing list has been obtained, the next step companies must undertake is to construct a message that will draw a response. This may be the most critical step in the entire marketing process. Online messages have to be shorter because online attention spans are short, particularly with e-mail.

One trick to cutting through the clutter filling a prospective customer's in-box is to personalize the e-mail, and make sure the heading is large. Just as in traditional e-mail, nothing works better than attention grabbers, and nothing grabs attention like a bold headline with a person's name in it.

There are other strategies that will improve return rates. If you have a clickable link, make sure the URL is placed twice in the body of the e-mail.

And if you have the e-mail signed by someone identifiable—say, a character from Sesame Street—the communication becomes personalized. It builds intimacy and makes it much easier to get to the meat of the message, which is, "buy my product!"

Another neat trick is to put a person's name in the "from" field of the e-mail. Again, it makes the communication more personal. A lot of companies will neglect that aspect, sending an e-mail from a weirdly named list-serving robot. That's a turnoff to potential customers.

With some sites, technology enables personalization to a far greater degree. If you have a clickable URL to a site that someone has visited before, filtering technology allows the site to recognize a customer and possibly offer a discount.

A textbook example of an effective online publicity campaign is the launch of Britannica.com, one of the most successful product introductions of a traditional brand into the online world.

We'll go into greater detail later in the book about the various aspects of the company and its attempts to recreate its two-centuries-old brand in the wired world. But let's talk now about its specific online efforts.

In the online publicity campaign for the launch of Britannica.com, the company decided to introduce its services in a very personal way. They began by directly providing information to individuals in the hopes that their discovery of a unique, new service would cause them to mention it to others, thus spreading the good word far beyond the reach of conventional media.

The campaign started off by literally going in to a randomly selected message board on history. There, someone had a posting trying to find out information about Queen Elizabeth.

The Britannica online marketing team would go back to the Britannica site, find information about the Queen, then take that specific URL back to the message board and say, "Hey, I saw that you're looking for information on Queen Elizabeth. I happened to go by Britannica.com and they have this great information on her. Here's the specific URL that you need to go to."

Yes, it's a very time-consuming technique. But it's cost effective. Those types of things can lead into other discussions and interaction, which is something a new product needs like plants need sunlight. In many cases these interactions can

Figure 10-2

snowball, just getting a product name out there, with that person then passing on word to their friends. The idea is to try to find interest that can be somehow tied in to the desire of the consumer.

A campaign for the environmental defenders Greenpeace is another example of a company that has waged highly effective campaigns to reach environmentally concerned citizens online. (See Figure 10-2.)

For a "Save the Whales" campaign, Greenpeace was concerned that whaling legislation was being set in other countries that would be detrimental to the long-term interests of whales. So a grassroots campaign was developed, encouraging online consumers to write letters to their Congressional representatives.

A special section was set up on the Greenpeace web site that people could go to and easily put in their name and zip code in a form they could automatically send to their representatives in Congress.

Much as in the Queen Elizabeth/Britannica campaign, the online marketing team for Greenpeace found people who had a particular interest in the environment and whaling and then used them to drive traffic to the site.

Activists went into newsgroups and message boards and homesteading sites like GeoCities and Xoom that were related to Greenpeace, and let them know what was going on with the whales. A lot of webmasters volunteered to put a link from their sites that would link back to the Greenpeace site, and it spread virally.

Often, the strategy for a company is to create and assist "online evangelists." Consumers with homesteading sites are very passionate about what they do. If they have a site on Ricky Martin, they want to do whatever they can to really promote him. Homesteading sites are a marketer's dream. The sites have proven extremely popular with Netizens, allowing them the space and tools to build their own web sites, free of charge. Such brands as GeoCities, Tripod, The Globe, Xoom, Fortune City, and AngelFire are among the Internet's most popular sites, with several offering millions of registered users.

Because the communities found at these URLs are so passionate, they are more than happy to participate in marketing campaigns. They will run news and links to webcasts, place photos, and do practically anything, merely for the thrill of being part of the insiders club helping their favorite cause, artist, or hobby.

Organized around specific general topics, the homesteading sites provide an easy way for marketers to identify a niche audience.

In the case of Greenpeace's marketing efforts, environmentalists were contacted to become part of the group's campaign. Naturally, anyone who took the time to put up a homesteading site tends to be very passionate, so they were largely very happy to help out and drive traffic to this particular initiative.

Again, remember—this must be very targeted. It's not enough to merely alert online users who have a GeoCities home page. A good viral publicity campaign must target users with a specific topic interest.

Be warned that problems can arise if businesses are careless in the way they communicate with their online audiences. In one particular example of such missteps, a direct e-mail campaign conducted by a B2B financial services company tried to reach targeted banks and small businesses. The company wanted to do a contest to try to attract a very select audience of business owners and banking professionals. They decided to give away a videotape because they happened to have copies of *Austin Powers: The Spy Who Shagged Me.*

The response rates were dismal and costly—a situation which could have been reconciled had the company created a customized incentive plan more appropriate for its target audience and tested the campaign with a small group of recipients first.

The lesson? It's important to make sure that incentivized audience interactions are targeted and complementary to an online business.

For example, if a business has a site that's selling stereos, it would not want to give away stereos. Strategically, it might want to give away CDs so that consumers would actually buy a stereo. One of the biggest problems with contests, not only online, but offline, is that people give away the wrong prize. Quite often, if it's not very targeted, a mass audience of online users will respond who are just interested in contests and sweepstakes, rather than developing a relationship with this company or its products.

Another key tactic in online publicity is search-engine optimization, or ensuring that the organization's web site or microsites are easy to find on search sites. Approximately 80 percent of all new web sites are found through the search engines. A quick peak at online survey numbers conducted by research firm Media Metrix reveals that all of the search-engine sites are up there in terms of site traffic volume, and most of them are within the top 10 most trafficked site index.

Search-engine optimization also embraces directories like Yahoo!, which are human edited. With directories, optimization is more about media relations, i.e., having a relationship with editors there, trying to get them listed in specific categories. Some companies have a team of full-time people who work on search-engine optimization, getting sites listed in directories and search engines. A lot of it is technical work, creating metatags, image-alt tags, inbound and outbound links, a lot of design issues.

Effective search-engine optimization can be time consuming and involves the coordination of design, technical, and marketing teams. But it's necessary because the way a search engine will rank a company's site is critical to being found by target audiences.

Site position in a search engine can actually vary quite significantly over the course of a week. A lot of that fluctuation is dependent upon the particular methodology of the search engine.

A site like Altavista will send out its "spider"—the electronic searching software that finds new sites—from every few days to every several weeks. Excite will send its out every 6 weeks, and Yahoo!, which uses human editors to determine search-engine position, doesn't change that often.

The Yahoo! editors are divided into specific categories, and not unlike media relations, a communicator must be familiar with the "editors" that supervise the different categories, who range in age from 20-somethings to the early 40s.

Before a company embarks on search-engine optimization, it is advisable for the design team to review its site and see what types of issues and hurdles there are to getting it listed.

There are a number of significant factors that go into that determination. If a new site is trying to get listed into Yahoo!, for example, the process can take up to 3 months and is not guaranteed to be successful.

A Yahoo! editor will review site information sent to him or her and make a determination whether the site will get indexed. If Yahoo! already has 200 sites on real estate, another real estate site might not get listed at all. It's quite arbitrary and in that sense not unlike media relations.

Search-engine optimization is about what that particular site editor wants at that particular time. While all search engines have different methodologies for ranking sites, they have some common factors. A lot of them are technical issues.

Search engines prefer very simple sites, without a lot of bells and whistles. A site with significant amounts of Flash animation does not carry high chances of getting listed because its competitor probably has a site that's very static and very search engine friendly. One of the first steps for any prospective online marketing team to take when deciding to work with a site is to examine its log files. See how much traffic they get from various search engines. That will determine how much positioning work is necessary to enhance the site's visibility on these crucial tools.

A good online marketing team will recognize some of the tricks of the trade right off the bat. For example, it is very important that a site have hypertext markup language (HTML) text on the home page that can be highlighted with a mouse.

Graphic text is skipped over by most search-engine robots, which are the invisible feelers sent out by most search sites to locate new pages for directory listings. That's why if you type a particular term into a search engine, all kinds of GeoCities home pages emerge. Most of those personal sites are pretty low tech. They load fast, they have a lot of HTML text, and often not a lot of graphics.

Another crucial design factor an online marketing team should recognize is whether or not a site uses frames. *Frames* are the name for the dividers that can segment a site into different windows.

If a site uses frames, they will deter the search engines from getting to the home page because the robot searches will not distinguish the various elements embedded into each window and put them into the big picture.

The other things to consider for optimal search-engine awareness are inbound and outbound links. In search engines like Google and DirectHit, their rankings are based on link popularity. So if an online user searches for "marketing," the first site that will come up is the most popular, or the site with the greatest number of inbound and outbound links for that term.

It is critical, but often an afterthought, to have links to other areas of the site and to include a site map. With a site map, a search engine spider is allowed to crawl the page much easier.

A big issue in search-engine optimization is database-generated sites. They spit out URLs that have special characters like question marks and plus signs. A search-engine robot can't read past the symbol, so the search engine will often truncate the URL.

It will still list the site, but it will truncate the URL to the part it can read. What that means is that when someone actually does try to access the site from a search-engine link, he or she will actually get an error message because that URL is part of a site, not an actual page. It's a constant challenge to coordinate all of these important factors when designing, refining, and promoting a web site.

Affiliate marketing is yet another great way to drive traffic to a site, with the added bonus of racking up sales.

Programs for affiliate marketing set up the equivalent of ministores throughout the Web that can help promote your products and services. Consumers opt in to become an affiliate of a CDNow or a Barnesandnoble.com, and agree to place links on their sites that will drive traffic. Any sales made from such traffic results in a commission to the affiliate.

Small and large businesses can develop affiliate program technology in house or go to a leading purveyor like BeFree, which will provide both the software and the back-end servicing of the programs.

Either personal home pages or business home pages work as affiliates, but almost all of them need some kind of content in order to be effective.

Affiliate programs need to be marketed in order to attract a large number of recruits. That can be achieved through direct e-mail, newsgroups, and message boards.

Internal marketing efforts also work well. Many companies have discovered that their best sales force is their existing customers. They've taken their existing database of customers and instituted things like Tell-a-Friend programs, where referrals get customers 10 percent off their next purchase.

Internet marketing has also spawned some businesses that are using their ability to drive traffic to sites to generate revenue.

GoTo.com, a paid-per-click service, is one effective company in the sector. Its business works like this: say you're a company selling mortgages online. You sign up with GoTo.com and agree to list yourself under the term "mortgage."

To obtain that keyword, you agree to pay GoTo.com $1.27 for each searcher that clicks through to your site based on his or her search. The problem for the mortgage company is that it can sink in the search-engine ratings by a higher bid. If another mortgage broker pays $1.28, they are ranked higher in the results.

Sites such as GoTo.com are effective in driving targeted traffic, and the site is highly monitored by a skilled team of editors, who are careful not to do things like selling porn terms to drive traffic to your particular e-commerce site. Because the traffic from such sites is preselected, studies have indicated it's very sticky. Plus, a "normal" search-engine listing can take months to obtain. GoTo.com can list a business instantaneously.

It's hard to market any business online, but it's particularly difficult to market B2B companies for two reasons: their services tend to have higher price points, and they are going after a very elusive, very specific audience.

In B2B marketing, it's not about how much traffic is coming to the site, it's about generating the right traffic. And it's really difficult to identify target audiences online. Although the situation is changing, the nascency of B2B online marketing requires new lists to be created, so B2B companies must first set up their own communities for their particular audiences. That means offering content that will bring them back.

If a business-to-business company wanted to reach *Fortune 500* CEOs, for example, it might set up a portion of its site containing all types of content that would interest that audience, possibly using a content-licensing service such as Screaming Media or iSyndicate. This, of course, would be done so that the company's name and background were placed prominently, enhancing brand awareness with that audience.

B2B aside, other companies have had difficulty establishing themselves with the online audience. Many companies have only themselves to blame, for they make it extremely difficult to do business.

Many companies make the mistake of asking up front for all sorts of registration information, which is a real deterrent to doing business with them. If a visitor wants to merely surf the site, they are required to submit a name and address, and the majority of online users don't want to give that information out so casually.

It's best to collect data over time. Yes, initially collecting names and e-mail addresses is innocent enough, but businesses must do so in a painless, opt-in way and adhere to the latest privacy policies. For example, any business can get a site user's name when he or she registers for a contest. Later, the business might ask for permission to market other items of interest if a site user makes a purchase. Gradually, as trust is established, a relationship develops that allows more data to be shared. This concept is generally known as *permission marketing*, a term and concept coined by Yoyodyne founder and author Seth Godin.

BMG, for all its success in viral marketing with Natalie Imbruglia, made the mistake of asking for a very long registration form in its initial foray on the Internet. As a result, BMG wasn't getting that many registered users at all. When BMG was advised of its error, it split up the registration form, just asking for name and e-mail address. The numbers skyrocketed.

E-mail is perhaps the perfect tool for public relations professionals, as it allows an intimate form of contact that mass media can't hope to duplicate.

That function is particularly effective when a public relations professional is using the tool with an established brand name. Let's now examine how it was used in one of the most successful site launches ever on the commercial Internet.

ONLINE INTELLIGENCE: THE CORNERSTONE TO TOP-NOTCH DIGITAL COMMUNICATIONS

Years ago, the world of public relations research often consisted of 6 months of focus groups followed by a large mailing of surveys that would come back with perceptions based on what happened 6 months ago. Today, the world of intelligence gathering and integration of offline and online research has totally reshaped the marketplace. Online intelligence's inherent advantage over traditional offline research is the speed with which the intelligence is not only gathered but also applied to ongoing communications strategy. For example, let's say a company has just launched a new online media room, and it wants to invite a certain group of journalists to evaluate the effectiveness of the media room. Instead of setting up appointments and waiting weeks for the various schedules to align, public relations professionals can now send these journalists an e-mail, and they can visit on their own time, be it Thursday at 9 p.m., Friday at 7:30 a.m., or whenever they want. By the end of 1 week, the communications team can receive most of the responses, an almost impossible time frame in the real world. Yes, online research is speedy, it's accessible, and it allows very quick, succinct feedback.

Online intelligence also allows an unprecedented direct glimpse at public opinion and sentiment—globally, cost effectively, and without the bias caused by a researcher asking questions in a well-lit room. This is achieved through monitoring chat rooms, online bulletin boards, and discussion groups. These resources allow an organization to simply and easily get a taste of how its company stacks up in certain audiences. For example, a quick look at job posting boards, career chats, and insider message boards can give a company a high-level understanding of how it is viewed as a potential workplace by prospective employees. The same holds true for those already employed. On some boards, current employees are encouraged to post the "real scoop" about their company, sometimes for free, other times for a stipend. Wondering why recruiting efforts have taken a dive? Maybe it's because the recent merger created a hostile environment within certain factions at the company. Or maybe employees consider new policies implemented by the company as akin to those at a sweatshop. The reality is that a business must acknowledge that most employees conduct some "guerrilla" online intelligence prior to interviewing or considering an offer from a potential employer. And any consumer, analyst, or journalist looking to get some real buzz on a company can easily tap into these free, global online focus groups.

Despite its advantages, companies have been slow to grasp the online edge, and often find information gathering in that manner a less credible research resource. In some cases, they are correct in their perceptions. There's no substitute for watching someone use a web site or having an offline conversation with study participants. But, on the other hand, online research has opened up a more global population of panelists. It's also created the means to get information in real time, and the ability to interact in an online focus group in a much more open way. When a study participant is sitting in a room full of focus-group participants, he or she might be less inclined to share a true opinion than with a faceless name online.

Online intelligence gathering really came into its own in the late 1990s, but the earliest firms began dabbling with it in the mid-1990s, when the first interactive panels were started. Today, some of the premier research firm panels total over 700,000 online households. Many of these panels are global, so they can tap into market segments in Australia, Japan, Europe, and Latin America as easily as they can in the United States. Panels are used in many ways, but the typical one would resemble a newsgroup chat. A moderator would ask a question and people would begin a discussion, with the panelists able to view each other's comments. At that point, the client company would be able to get instant feedback and interact with the moderator in real time. So, for example, if the company was thinking about introducing a new cell phone, the panel might be asked some basic questions about their use of the phone: Is it comfortable to hold? Does it fit snugly in its case? Is a speed-dialing button desirable? Upon reviewing the answers, the client could then follow up with a related question, perhaps directing the moderator to ask the study participants about the color of the phone or other features. The questions and answers would flow back and forth until the desired amount of information had been elicited.

The key today is the application of the kind of intelligence gained from primary or secondary, quantitative or qualitative research. Digital public relations has no room for research for research's sake. This leads to a key point: different companies have different needs in online intelligence. New companies entering a marketplace need to know how they're perceived, how their competitors are perceived, and what's going on in their marketplaces. It's important for them to take a snapshot of the potential audiences for their products before they get involved in the marketplace. More traditional companies have a different set of problems. Already established in the market, they need to analyze new sets of competitors and a constantly changing audience. Whether they're launching a new product, or they're trying to transition from being a big, fat, dumb company to being perceived as cool, smart, savvy and fast company, they need to know what the business landscape is and where they fit in.

Competitive intelligence in public relations focuses on the communications strategies, positioning, messaging, and new techniques that a competitor is using to differentiate its brand and create category ownership. This kind of intelligence is best gained through a combination of secondary and primary research, and should be used to continuously feed and evaluate a business's communications strategies. In public relations, competitive intelligence is used to provide context, evaluate legitimacy, and identify new opportunities for category ownership or development.

With established companies, their online intelligence teams might start out a revised branding initiative, for example, by conducting an image analysis. In the analysis, the team would use all available online information—including newsgroups, chat groups, and message boards—and take a snapshot of a company's image in time, along with suggestions. The image analysis is used to quickly assess and attack a problem, answering the most basic questions: Where has the company been, what's working, and what's not working? An analysis of the information could yield answers to questions like, "How can I differentiate my brand in the marketplace?" and "How does the Internet business media perceive the challenges my company faces in building a sustainable business model?"

Table 11-1   Ten Things You Can Learn from Online Intelligence

How is your company being perceived by consumers, employees, and the media?

Is your communications program effectively reaching the online audience?

What kinds of business and consumer issues are your constituencies following?

How are your competitors positioning themselves?

What kinds of messages are being received about you and your competitors in the industry?

How does your web site stack up against the competition?

What do your web site visitors think about your brand? Your site? Their overall experience with your company online?

Who are your online audiences and how do they wish to interact with you online?

Has your brand image changed over time? How do you stack up with the competition?

How can you build and enhance your brand via communications offline and online?

Nowhere is online intelligence more essential than in the launch of a new brand. (See Table 11-1.) A multinational accounting firm was going to spin off one of its business units to begin offering an employee portal for companies to reach out to their employees with discounts and incentives. Prior to launching, the new company conducted a competitive market analysis to understand what the perceptions of the company were, especially negative ones it would need to shed with a new rebranding, and to identify the challenges and opportunities presented in the new marketplace it was entering. The company's launch team identified a number of issues they would need to address prior to launch, issues this company had never needed to address prior to the new spin-off. One issue was privacy and how the company's new service would abide by standards established by leaders in the online privacy arena. The second issue uncovered from the study was how this new business would fit into the overall category of online work life management—a new, business-critical issue for companies around the world. Based on this analysis, the company refined its positioning, placing a heavier emphasis on its groundbreaking privacy protection technology and the wider scope of its new offering that excelled the evolution of online work life solutions.

Speed is essential to an image analysis, and its results need to be acted on with equal haste. Online intelligence is also optimally provided on an ongoing basis to reflect the rapidly changing marketplace. It is not uncommon for research, strategy, and implementation activities to take place simultaneously in fast-moving environments. Some have made a mistake with placing too much emphasis on one or the other at the sake of another critical component. Strategy, intelligence, and implementation act like a three-legged stool for most rapidly changing businesses. A company that made the mistake of emphasizing implementation over strategy and intelligence, getting caught up in its launch campaign, was a B2B marketplace provider. The company commissioned a competitive market snapshot in order to develop refined positioning in the e-marketplace–builder arena. When the analysis had been conducted and the strategy had been developed, key executives were too busy doing other things to step back and evaluate the results of the intelligence-gathering exercise and update their strategy. When they were finally ready, the intelligence was 2 months old, and in the B2B marketplace 2 months can be like 2 years, which resulted in outdated strategy. Smart companies are using intelligence gathering to take action, a change from the days when researching and researching and researching was the modus operandi.

U.S. companies are becoming particularly adept at this speeded-up world. In Japan, there's more of a problem. So much analysis and research is conducted that no one ever takes action, the classic analysis/paralysis paradigm. The ideal use of image analysis is to very quickly discard the company's inefficiencies and very quickly identify the things that are working. Then a communications strategy can be developed or refined with this new intelligence.

What intelligence really comes down to is branding. If one looks at the keys to branding through public relations today, three key points—metrics, leadership, and lexicon—intelligence gathering is central to all of them. Intelligence provides the platform for differentiation that can be communicated within three key points, supported by industry-standardized metrics. Intelligence gathering can identify opportunities and challenges for leadership and/or perhaps ways to develop a new category so that leadership is ensured. And lastly, intelligence provides insight into the nomenclature that is paramount for positioning. Competitive intelligence gathering is like a standard safety technique in a burning building—you must feel a door to see if it's hot before opening it—and if it is, you must find another way out. To do otherwise is to risk getting burned. In short, for a brand to build credibility and adapt to changing market forces, intelligence must become an essential component of a communicator's toolbox.

New forays into online intelligence gathering have also added a whole new world of competitive data-gathering tools and methods. Today, most corporate web sites are ample fodder for competitive research. Coupled with online SEC filings, financial information, an archive of press releases, new hires, job postings, online buzz, and business intelligence from credible sites like Hoover's, competitive intelligence gathering has never been easier. One technique used by Internet-savvy public relations professionals is to search by a competitor's name in the search engines to see what kind of information comes up.

One way to add a robust volume of competitive intelligence is to enlist the help of an online clipping service, such as Net Currents or eWatch, to monitor your business and your competitors. News clipping services available through "custom clips" on the Dow Jones Interactive Service can also help by downloading all relevant information on the companies to be monitored in one quickly accessible page. Other services, such as Company Sleuth, will provide a brief, daily snapshot of a company's image via how many new message-board postings have appeared, new press releases, and news coverage. The company will also monitor new domain names that have been registered, a particularly useful early-warning system that can spot competitors months before they begin to show up on a company's radar. For a great chuckle, Internet users can see how many companies have registered "their own name-sucks.com" to prevent cyberattacks. (See Table 11-2.)

Table 11-2   Excellent Resources for Competitive Intelligence Online

YOUR COMPETITORS' WEB SITES	EVERYWHERE!
SEC filings	http://www.sec.gov
Hoover's	http://www.hoovers.com
Company Sleuth	http://www.companysleuth.com
Dow Jones Company Clips	http://www.djinteractive.com
Emarketer	http://www.emarketer.com
Vault.com	http://www.vault.com
Insight Express	http://www.insightexpress.com
Fuld Internet Intelligence Index	http://www.fuld.com
AIM Research	http://www.interactivehq.com
Net Currents	http://www.netcurrents.com
@Brint (Business Researcher's Interests)	http://www.brint.com

To gather direct image-assessment information, companies can also use the assistance of quantitative market research houses. NFO is known as the largest consumer panel in the world and the pioneer of consumer research, having started consumer panels over 50 years ago in the prewired world. It reaches more than 1.6 million people nationwide, roughly translating into 1 out of every 170 households in the United States. The company's NFO Interactive arm provides an e-mail survey that rewards participants and referral contacts with prizes as an incentive to complete panel surveys. For example, users receive $2.00 for each and every eligible person they refer, and, as an extra bonus, $5.00 is paid for every five people that are referred during a given quarter. When participants are asked questions, their personal information is held in confidence and is not released to any outside parties. That gives users an added sense of security and assurance, resulting in candid answers that greatly benefit a client. The benefits of using NFO research for conducting online panels is that a vast sample of the American population is surveyed, resulting in a cross section of ideas, values, and opinions. Other interactive research services are provided by Greenfield Online and FIND/SVP.

Another new online research tool is Vault.com. The site provides potential employees, company insiders, current employees, recruiters, and researchers information on specific companies and industries via message boards, news boards, and job postings areas. Additional industry information is given through suggestions for books, experts, and recruiting services. Specific industries covered on Vault.com include consulting, technology, venture capitalists, and law. Vault.com is an accurate snapshot of the career and company market space because real employees are sharing their real and honest experiences. In May 2000, Vault.com hit a milestone, as its message board had its 100,000th posting. (See Table 11-3 for the most popular areas of Vault.com.)

Deja.com is clearly representative of a "window" into online consumer opinion. It is an outlet for consumers to view others' ratings, opinions, and discussions on products, lifestyle, and travel.

Table 11-3

TOP INDUSTRIES TALKED ABOUT ON VAULT.COM (AS OF JULY 2000)
Investment banking
Management consulting
Law
Internet and new media
High tech

TOP COMPANIES TALKED ABOUT ON VAULT.COM (AS OF JULY 2000)
Andersen Consulting
Goldman Sachs
Morgan Stanley Dean Witter
McKinsey
Metropopolitan Life

Users visit Deja.com to gain additional insight and information on competitive prices, competitive features, and current user response to the product before actually making a purchase. On the Deja.com site, ratings, discussion boards, reviews, product descriptions, and comparison tools can be found.

Numerous sites have popped up that solicit consumer opinion, most prominently Epinions, a site that contains opinions on over 100,000 products and services in order to guide buying decisions. The company has set up an entire page on each company mentioned, featuring a collection of news articles, write-ins, and rankings. (See Figure 11-1.)

Online intelligence can also be used to evaluate existing communications strategies, notably online public relations tactics such as online media rooms and crisis management programs. Too many companies are only evaluating their web sites from a consumer point of view. That's not enough. To be successful, companies must also evaluate their sites as though the media were their customers.

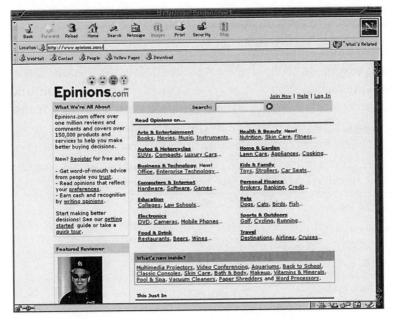

Figure 11-1

Companies that understand the need to accommodate the media's access on their web site realize enormous benefits.

First, they get much better, in-depth coverage of their businesses and their positions in their specific business niches. Almost all of the media that cover a company use its web site as the first place to get the background information necessary to construct a proper interview.

The media's needs are much different from that of a consumer. When they arrive at a site, media people are not looking for whizbang and flash.

Instead, they prefer that site information is up to date, accurate, and easy to find. Yet many are surprised at the number of companies that treat their online pressrooms as an afterthought. It's almost like they've just tacked it on. "Oh, yeah. We forgot! Our public relations firm said we had to have a pressroom."

That attitude translates to the media in a highly negative way, making it almost impossible to get to the right information, which results in negative connotations of the corporate image.

Positioning a business as a category leader in the Internet business space isn't going to ring true if the company's last posted online press release was from February of the year before.

Good corporate web sites convey accurate, up-to-date information. They allow a reporter to access more information and ask better questions. Make a reporter's life easier, and it'll translate to a much better experience for both sides.

It happens every day in the public relations agency business. A company complains that a reporter doesn't understand the company or its business. "They ask dumb questions," is a common refrain.

The truth is that a public relations specialist can easily prevent this type of reaction. If public relations representatives would allow the media and analyst community to get better information on the company, it is almost guaranteed that better questions will be asked.

In the early days of the online world, some public relations people used to get asked simple questions by reporters: What is the name of your company? What do you do? And similar contextual questions.

But by the late 1990s, journalists were using corporate web sites as a reference tool, and companies noticed a change. They were being asked intelligent and provocative questions because reporters found information online.

To ensure a company's web site is effectively reaching the media, companies should be proactive. Solicit online opinion from the media on how easy the site is to navigate, and ask whether the information is meeting their needs. Use site traffic figures to evaluate where users go online, and determine whether low-trafficked areas can be better positioned on the site. (See Table 11-4.)

One of the best uses of an online media room has been undertaken by Boeing, which has a long history of needing to respond to crisis situations, comment on industry issues, and maintain relationships with several categories of media and industry influencers. Boeing has two levels of access to its online media room, one for consumers and other site visitors and another for registered media. The password-protected area

Table 11-4   Basic Ingredients for an Effective Media Room Online

Content	Is it updated frequently?
	Is new information easy to find?
	Is contact information readily available?
	Is the information comprehensive?
User experience	Is the site easy to find? From the company's home page, is news easily accessible?
	Is the password-accessible area easy to use and valuable?
Features	Does the site feature downloadable images and photos?
	Does the site feature video and audio footage?
	Does the site feature links and other noncorporate resources?
Functionality	Can the media easily search the site?
	Can the media access news via e-mail, PDA, cell phone?
	Can the media e-mail a question or request and get a swift response?

contains updated company statements, images of planes, maps, biographies, contact information, available video footage, and answers to many frequently asked questions regarding a wide variety of subjects at Boeing.

That's what journalists are looking for: an answer. Recently, a financial services company used focus groups comprised of media and public relations associates experienced in developing media sites in order to develop an online media room. By tapping into what their specific audience wanted prior to developing the site, the company saved a lot of time, money, and effort and was able to phase out the development of the media site into high- and low-priority items. Another not-for-profit organization was not so lucky. They evaluated their site immediately following a lengthy development cycle and discovered that the flashy graphics they had paid for so dearly were "too bright, confusing, and childish" to their online news audience.

Want a good horror story on the effects of not researching your market? Look at some of the inevitable dot-com failures sprinkling the landscape. Examine Boo.com, the ill-fated sportswear site marketed with an extreme attitude. Among other things, the company's market research should have shown that a some-what snobbish, overly sophisticated persona, combined with a Macintosh-unfriendly interface unavailable in Europe, made everyone feel that they weren't cool enough to ever become a regular visitor, much less a customer. If this company had talked to even a couple of its customers, or looked at how the user experience was being understood and communicated by the media, there's no way that it would have made those mistakes.

As a result, Boo.com was not filling a marketing need, and soon found itself out of cash, unable to raise more money. The company missed a basic point: no one needs to shop at a site with a terrible, slow interface that is not Macintosh-compliant and has a major attitude. And no firm can afford not to know what its customers and potential customers are thinking.

Now that you have some of the secrets of gathering and leveraging online intelligence, let's examine one of the biggest tests of these theories ever conducted—transitioning a famous offline brand into the dot-com world.

A CASE STUDY OF ONLINE SUCCESS: BRITANNICA.COM

The new world of today's public relations can be seen through one paramount case study: the relaunch of *Encyclopaedia Britannica* as an online brand (see Figure 12-1). *Encyclopaedia Britannica* was the Internet's first 231-year-old start-up. In 1997, after more than two centuries as the world's leading reference source, *Encyclopaedia Britannica* found itself losing ground to online information sites.

A new ownership group, led by a member of the Edmond Safra family, purchased the company with the goal of transforming Britannica into a major Internet brand.

The company needed transforming. In short, these folks were in trouble. In fact, their business was later used as a case study in a book by the Boston Consulting Group as the prime example of a company that could have lost its business as a result of the Internet.

By the mid-1990s, it was obvious that electronic information was the wave of the future, and Britannica found book sales declining dramatically, despite its reputation as the world's leading encyclopedia.

To combat these losses, the company entered the CD-ROM market and offered several services to allow users to access its content online if they paid a fee.

But the CD-ROMs sold modestly. It soon became apparent that Britannica's future would hinge on the success of a broadly

Figure 12-1

focused consumer portal. That's when they turned to public relations.

The company already had some idea of what it wanted to do. With an investment of millions of dollars, it had begun to produce a web site. However, as the company has admitted many times, it had no idea how to market the web site.

But the company at least knew it needed top-quality public relations and advertising. In the end, that proved to be the company's edge.

The Britannica team faced an uphill battle to understand the Internet on numerous fronts.

Even the company's work environment bespoke a "doesn't get it" attitude, in that its building was an old traditional building on West Michigan Avenue, prime real estate in Chicago, but miles away from the type of environment that most fast-paced Internet start-ups thrive on. Wide hallways, old-fashioned paneling—clearly it was not physically an office environment that looked or felt like an Internet company.

Secondly, the people involved, while really smart and knowledgeable, wore suspenders, French cuffs with cufflinks, and starched white shirts. These were not your typical young kids who grew up with computers since grade school.

These were senior people, for the most part, who had very successful careers, but who now found themselves compelled to move into this space. They clearly didn't have the look of an Internet company, and they certainly didn't have the culture of one.

Not only did the company need to create a good marketing plan but it also needed to "get it." The staff needed to be indoctrinated into the culture of the Internet so that they began to really live it, breathe it, eat it, sleep it, enjoy it. Only by doing that could they truly understand what was driving the market and what their customers wanted.

Britannica had zero margin for error. If it did not figure out quickly what the Internet meant, it was in danger of losing everything.

The primary focus of the campaign was to position Britannica.com as a strong and relevant online brand and a leading source of knowledge on the Internet, with the goal of driving traffic to the site.

To achieve that, the company pinned the success of the launch entirely on the public relations campaign. The advertising campaign was not scheduled to start until December, 3 months after the outgoing PR effort began in September. Public relations would have to blaze the trail and generate the attention that would compliment the advertising campaign. Bottom line: everything was riding on public relations.

The actual launch of Britannica.com presented several challenges. Although the encyclopedia's market (including Britannica's CD-ROMs) caters primarily to schools and libraries, the new site would need to have a mass consumer appeal.

At the same time, research showed that Britannica.com was likely to be compared to established portal sites such as Yahoo! and About.com. Thus, the focus of the agency public relations campaign was to stay away from these direct juxtapositions while also avoiding pigeonholing as a niche information site catering to academic audiences.

The main objective was to position the company as a unique offering, rather than as yet another entry in a crowded playing field.

The agency's first step was to conduct a full analysis of Britannica's position in the marketplace, both offline and on the Internet, and to assess the competitive landscape of information web sites. The agency needed the lay of the land to uncover exactly what was going on in the marketplace and to pinpoint who, in fact, were the company's competitors.

A thorough competitive analysis examined all the major portals that would be competitive to Britannica, and outlined the company's pros and cons in comparison to its rivals.

Because Britannica was providing a search engine and an archive, the competitive study focused on companies that were already established sites where people went for knowledge, search engines like Altavista, Yahoo!, and Excite.

The question posed was how Britannica was going to compete with these already established outlets? First to market is a decided edge in the wired world. How would Britannica differentiate itself from its competitors and lure audience share? What were some of the issues that the media would look at?

The answer to those questions surprised the Britannica team.

One of the key things identified during this phase of the analysis was that the company's business model was going to get the most scrutiny. The executives had thought that the actual features of the portal were going to be the difference, the fact that "we have a better search engine and more text."

But they were told that the biggest amount of coverage anticipated upon launch were questions about where the business was going. Where would Britannica fit in the wired world of today and in the future?

Britannica needed to be able to address that in a way that set it apart from its competition going forward. It needed to know the language and the industry standards of successful, new revamped business models.

While it was trailing the field, Britannica was providing large amounts of original content through its editors. These were serious researchers and writers, capable of delivering extremely valuable and reliable information online.

That was something that the other search engines couldn't match. They were aggregators of information. Britannica was both an aggregator and an originator of content.

To make its package even more enticing, Britannica made a very good offer to potential consumers. It was going to put the entire encyclopedia online for free. The company had a number of economic models on how to make money if it did that.

Based on the results of that research, Britannica was presented with a position that would serve as a concise articulation of the company's vision for the site: Britannica.com is the most trusted source of information, knowledge, and learning on the Internet, provided free of charge. It's the web portal for smart people.

The time prior to the September launch was used to provide a steady stream of market information to Britannica, not just as it related to its web site, but also in terms of how it affected the entire Internet industry. The information was presented in a variety of ways, including one-on-one sessions with key executives.

At the same time, the public relations team began building a program that was designed to allow Britannica to compete with other portals that had been around longer, had a large mind share of the target audience, and had bigger advertising budgets.

The overall objective was to create awareness. This was a brand-new portal, and no one associated the Encyclopaedia Britannica Company as actually being an Internet company. So the company had to be transformed in the public's mind into an Internet company.

In effect, the company was transitioning from a big, fat, dumb company to an e-business. And that is a situation that is applicable to many, many, many clients in many types of businesses.

The company had to differentiate the Britannica brand. To do that, industry issues were identified that Britannica could own, all designed to plant the seed in people's minds that Britannica gets what's going on in the business. After that, it would be easier to use the offer of the encyclopedia as the primary promotion, targeting mothers, the educational community, and kids.

Everyone wants to be with a winner, to stay on the cutting edge. Clearly, Britannica was going to be on that edge.

At the same time the campaign to consumers was formulated, Britannica editors and the subjects that they covered were introduced to the media. That was designed to position Britannica's editors as being above and beyond what's typically found not only on other web sites but also in many other news-oriented sites.

The editors were portrayed as stars, valuable resources available to the consumers and the media. In short, Britannica.com was touted as the most trusted source of information, knowledge, and learning on the Internet, provided free of charge.

The first step toward achieving differentiation between Britannica and its competitors was to train the company's three main spokespeople to avoid using words like "portal" or "encyclopedia" to the media.

Instead, the goal was to position Britannica.com as a new model for information on the Internet, rather than as a rehashed version of Yahoo! or Encarta. The press materials highlighted a fusion of traditional knowledge and the new world of the Internet. That was what Britannica truly represented. A bold, new service for a bold, new age.

The plan was to maintain a very low profile until launch, when the gloves were going to come off. Launch was going to mean everything for this product, and Britannica needed to maximize its exposure at that point.

There was a time not long ago when anybody would cover the news of a new launch. Now, with hundreds of new web sites debuting each month, it's much tougher. But if you can make your site's launch into an event, if you can make it exciting and come up with a new angle, launches are still a news-making opportunity.

To bolster the chances of that happening, the public relations agency conducted an analyst tour in September, including stops at Jupiter, Forrester, Aberdeen and Gomez, among other top research firms.

After these visits, a number of prominent endorsements from the analysts were obtained, which were then parlayed to the media during the launch.

To top off the launch-day campaign, exclusive interviews were offered to *The Wall Street Journal* and CNN's Garrick Utley for stories to appear on the launch day.

The CNN feature ran in rotation throughout the day, and *The Wall Street Journal* story ran in every edition of the paper. Also, 37 launch-day interviews were set up with a variety of outlets, including every major wire service, National Public Radio, *The Chicago Tribune*, CBS radio, NBC News, *The New York Times*, MSNBC, and online publications including C/NET, ZDNews, and Internet.com. By the end of the first week, more than 60 interviews had been arranged. In addition, public relations specialists were brought on board in the United Kingdom to handle the launch throughout Europe.

The initial Britannica agenda called for advertising to follow 2 weeks after launch. Public relations was going to plant the seed, get the editorial, get people to have some awareness, and then advertising was going to drive home the message and the image.

October 1999 marked the introduction of Britannica.com, a free destination site containing all 44 million words in the venerable 32-volume encyclopedia. The site also featured news feeds from over 80 magazines and newspapers, weather, sports scores, and a web search engine.

As planned, there were exclusives in *The Wall Street Journal*, *Business Week*, and Reuters on the day of launch. That started an incredible run of press attention, which resulted in over 600 stories that ran in the United States alone over the course of the next few weeks.

But the overwhelming attention also had an unexpected consequence. There was so much demand that Britannica servers were overloaded. The client was unprepared for the number of people trying to access the site, which immediately crashed.

The situation was now in crisis. Journalists were calling and asking, "Well, where's the site? We're seeing construction signs. I thought you guys were up."

A 25-year-old public relations associate came up with the perfect solution. Journalists and anyone else who was interested in listening were told that the demand validated the success of the model.

It was a very simple idea—most brilliant ideas are simple—and right on target. The point was credible and understandable, and everybody bought it.

Although the site was down longer than it should have been, almost 10 days, the demand held.

As a result of the public relations campaign, Britannica.com was "crippled by user volume," according to CNET. *The Wall Street Journal* reported that more than 12 million users logged on to the site during its first day, crashing the servers. Associated Press called the flow of traffic to the site "a tidal wave," and labeled Britannica "a victim of huge user demand." *USA Today* said "users have already swamped the site," and Wired News credited the launch with "drawing in tons of traffic."

Even the BBC got into the act, calling Britannica.com "one of this year's most touted Internet site launches." Frankly, because the site was down so long, it got to the point where, if they were down much longer, they would never capture all of the people who were ready to sign up.

However, when it did return, it proved to be another media opportunity. "Britannica's back up" said the headlines. There was a second bite at the apple.

The launch was so successful that the advertising scheduled to begin 2 weeks after the site debuted was constantly pushed back. Because demand was so huge, it didn't make any sense to advertise.

Eventually, the company wound up selling a lot of their Christmas slots on the open spot market. For the year 2000, what was going to be a $22 million ad budget was cut back to $17 million. The public relations budget, which was on the order of $500,000, was nearly doubled.

Because of the overwhelming debut, the president of the firm, Don Yannias, went from a skeptic about the value of public relations to a total convert. He now believes that public relations is going to continue to be the driving force that builds the Britannica brand.

To date, more than 1000 print articles and 200 television and radio broadcasts about Britannica.com have appeared in the United States, including feature stories in dozens of newspapers including *The Chicago Tribune, The Wall Street Journal, The New York Times, The Los Angeles Times*, and *USA Today*.

The New York Times referred to Britannica's launch as "arguably the most successful in the history of the Internet."

The Britannica model can be adopted by other companies, no matter what business they're in.

The first lesson: the launch is a news-making opportunity not to be missed. It should be done on an international basis. And there has to be a great offer.

Yes, it helps a lot when you also have brand recognition. Let's face it, even though *Encyclopedia Britannica* was not thought of as an Internet company, it helped that everyone knew who Britannica was. Combine that with a great offer and a great communications program, and the results broke the bank.

But even if you have some of those elements but not all, you can still use this sort of campaign. Many companies launch without all of the elements. Many of the dot coms didn't have the luxury of starting with a brand name, so they needed to create some news. That led to dot coms doing some flamboyant things, like having bungee jumpers or people flying out of airplanes, the most hysterical events. It's all designed to create some news and attention.

That's also why much of the dot-com advertising in the early stages was so off the wall. It had to be in order to get anyone to pay attention to them. But as we have now stated many times, much of that advertising was totally worthless, as it failed to cut through the clutter or, worse, merely confused consumers.

Had that money been used for public relations, it would have produced a better result. As we've seen with Britannica, public relations drives site launches.

Clearly, Britannica's success was measurable in that you could count the number of visitors and the amount of press. And, of course, they displaced the real-world product.

But there are other ways to measure public relations success. It's a question agencies are asked all the time. The answer is one of the reasons why public relations has been so successful, i.e., it has gone from an art form that could not be measured, other than a feel, to a form that is a combination of art and science that can be measured.

One measurement tool the larger companies will use is extensive research to test awareness levels. This is very expensive, and this is more typical of what ad agencies will do, testing awareness and perception levels prior to the start of a campaign.

If they are used, tests should be done at the start of the campaign, and then repeated every quarter to make sure that the trend, the awareness levels, and the positive perception levels go up.

But there are other tangible ways to measure success without spending money on research.

One easy way to see how public relations is working is to watch how 800-number calls increase. It's a common phenomenon. When a major executive appears on CNN, or has a major piece in *The Wall Street Journal*, the 800-number rings off the hook. It's public relations at work, driving new inquires whose interest in a company was tweaked by the news.

Another, obvious measure of success is tracking hits to a web site. You should be able to track how many unique visitors come to a site, what part of the site they visit, what time of day they went to it, and the number of people who registered, the latter most critical because that's how you build your databases.

A less immediate, but no less effective, measure of public relations at work is tracking the number of news articles that are published over time, the size of those articles, and the success of the articles in positioning the message points.

It's one thing to have a story, but it's another to have one that covered your key message points. Did it cover them in a clear and understandable way or was it a negative piece? Either way, it will have an effect that will tell you how your public relations campaign is doing.

There is one other measure of success, and it's the most obvious of all. If there's an e-commerce component to your campaign, sales levels will tell you everything you need to know about how well your public relations is working.

But the biggest overall lesson about online marketing is one that should ensure its vitality far into the future.

In most cases, marketing on the Internet exceeds expectations every time. You can make projections, but when it's done right, the amount of people who will come to your business, who will get excited, who will spend time on the site, who can travel around the site, who will talk to their friends, who in peak season will spend money, is nothing short of amazing.

The Internet is truly a worldwide forum, a forum in which you have people who love it, people who are really, truly into it, embracing it with a passion that's rarely equaled in other media. It's a fact. People are now online more than they're watching television. While that's good news, there is no textbook for reaching this type of market. People are experimenting, and, inevitably, there's going to be a lot of miserable failures. But there's also going to be an enormous number of successes.

What we're seeing now is some tried and true techniques beginning to emerge so programs can be built comfortably, with reasonable expectation of success. We're truly on the path of creating a wonderful new medium, one that will potentially unite the planet's commerce and culture in ways that we cannot even begin to predict.

The future belongs to those who understand this wired world. I hope you will use the lessons we've outlined to become a part of that story.

CONCLUSION: WHAT THE FUTURE HOLDS

If Gordon Moore can't figure it out, how can I?

Moore was the fellow who founded Intel along with Andy Grove. He came up with something called Moore's law. Essentially, it says that chip speed will double every 18 months.

He was correct for about 18 months.

Now chip speed doubles almost every 9 months. Moore himself now says he was too conservative, although, at the time, he was pilloried for his brazen predictions.

Today, according to researchers at the University of California at Los Angeles and Hewlett-Packard, chips can be made out of atoms. Smaller than white blood cells, they may be powered by human body heat.

Who could have imagined such a development? And who among us in the early 1990s could have imagined the sea of change in communications brought about by the Internet?

Nothing has ever so radically and fundamentally changed the way public relations professionals conduct their jobs. Our economy is now about information. Content is key. We're about conducting a dialogue with customers by whatever means necessary. Integrating communications is not a trite term but a marketplace necessity. Smart businesses now want one strategy conducted over many marketing disciplines. They want one brand voice, one brand equity, and, certainly, one budget to achieve that aim.

What matters most to today's company is that money is apportioned to those areas shown to be most effective in delivering its brand objectives.

No longer does advertising automatically get the lion's share of the marketing budget. In fact, by some estimates, 70 percent of all marketing budget funds go to nonmedia communications, a reverse proportion to a decade ago.

So what's next for public relations?

What follows is an attempt to give some perspective on where things are going. Like Gordon Moore, I expect I'll be too conservative.

THE INTERNET WILL CEASE TO EXIST

At least as a distinct communications tool. Because it will be everywhere and since we will be constantly connected, people will not think, "Now I'll go to the Internet." Phones, hand-held devices, televisions, and PCs will merge into single systems, always connected to a network, 24 hours, 7 days a week. The consequence of that will be that distinct public relations programs for different mediums will disappear. There will be one medium, the Internet, with multiple channels. It will be everything we have and can imagine wrapped into one.

ADVERTISING AGENCIES AS WE KNOW THEM WILL BE DEAD

They will be replaced by communications agencies. Advertising is an intrusive device. Today, when your TV show stops and an ad goes on the tube, you either watch the ad or go to the kitchen or bathroom.

That game is over.

With the Internet, you can go anywhere at any time. Formal commercials won't work. Remember, it's all about content. The Internet was made for public relations, for it's a tool driven by content, unlike advertising, which is image-oriented. Advertising, once king of the roost, is now but one of many communications tools, some of which have greater importance to the client.

In the future, the communications agency will understand how the various communications disciplines mix. And that agency will be positioned to serve clients as needs change.

GLOBALIZATION WILL RULE

The Internet, the place where we all come together but where no one rules is no longer the exclusive domain of the United States. A spring 2000 report by IDC, an Internet research firm, predicts that two-thirds of all e-commerce spending will take place outside the country by 2003. In that year, IDC says, consumer spending on web sites in the United States will reach $119 billion, but overseas sites will garner $209 billion of business. Large, irrepressible forces are reshaping the globe, led by the Internet and the Information Age. The moment you log onto the Internet you can communicate virtually for free anywhere in the world. Thanks to the Internet we have one postal system, one shopping mall, one library, one college, one world. It has gone from a curiosity to becoming the essential tool of our planet.

THE DIGITAL DIVIDE WILL UNITE

Our world will unite as the cost of computer ownership becomes available for almost everyone. Already we are seeing huge swings in Internet usage demographics. For a long time, the image of the typical Internet user was the heterosexual white male younger than 40. Although this characterization was mostly true, the Internet is now becoming a thriving marketplace for a wider range of people.

A MARKETING ASSET ALLOCATION OFFICER WILL EMERGE

Communications budgets are often the biggest expense items for digital companies. As we write in the summer of 2000, there is a huge need in many companies for someone who can wisely allocate budgets across multiple disciplines. That same officer will also be responsible for determining return on marketing investment (ROMI).

COMMUNICATIONS OFFICERS WILL JOIN BOARDS OF DIRECTORS

We're just beginning to see some action in that area now, but by 2005 the communications officer will sit on boards in numbers proportionate to the current number of attorneys, consultants, and others who populate them.

PRIVACY WILL BE LOST

Sad, but true. It will be impossible to keep data on viewing and purchasing patterns isolated. And finally.

THE WORLD WILL BE A BETTER PLACE

As communications brings down formal borders we will become more of a single world.

Information will flow freely, making us all more humane as the barriers that now separate us slip away into the dustbin of history.

I couldn't be more optimistic or excited.

INDEX

ABOUT THE AUTHOR

Don Middleberg is the chairman and CEO of Middleberg Euro, the fastest-growing public relations agency in the country for the past two years, with offices in New York, San Francisco, and Boston. A leader in public relations and marketing, Middleberg is widely considered to be among the elite communications professionals in digital public relations. A noted author and lecturer, he is coauthor of the groundbreaking Middleberg/Ross Media in Cyberspace Study. Middleberg is regularly called upon for commentary by numerous magazines and newspapers and has appeared on CNBC, C/Net, CNN, and National Public Radio.